the Softball Drill Book

KIRK WALKER

EDITOR

Human Kinetics

Library of Congress Cataloging-in-Publication Data

The softball drill book / Kirk Walker, editor.
   p. cm.
  ISBN-13: 978-0-7360-6070-7 (soft cover)
  ISBN-10: 0-7360-6070-7 (soft cover)
  1. Softball--Training.   2. Softball--Coaching.   I. Walker, Kirk 1965-
  GV881.4.T72S64 2007
  796.357'8--dc22

                                            2006102065

ISBN-10: 0-7360-6070-7
ISBN-13: 978-0-7360-6070-7

Acquisitions Editor: Jana Hunter; **Developmental Editor:** Amanda Eastin; **Assistant Editor:** Christine Horger; **Copyeditor:** John Wentworth; **Proofreader:** Darlene Rake; **Graphic Designer:** Bob Reuther; **Graphic Artist:** Sandra Meier; **Photo Manager:** Neil Bernstein; **Cover Designer:** Keith Blomberg; **Photographer:** Ryan Gardner; **Art Manager:** Kelly Hendren; **Illustrator (cover):** Andrew Tietz; **Illustrator (interior):** Al Wilborn; **Printer:** Versa Press

We thank Oregon State University in Corvallis, Oregon, for assistance in providing the location for the photo shoot for this book.

Human Kinetics books are available at special discounts for bulk purchase. Special editions or book excerpts can also be created to specification. For details, contact the Special Sales Manager at Human Kinetics.

Printed in the United States of America

10 9 8 7 6 5 4 3 2 1

Human Kinetics
Web site: www.HumanKinetics.com

United States: Human Kinetics
P.O. Box 5076
Champaign, IL 61825-5076
800-747-4457
e-mail: humank@hkusa.com

Canada: Human Kinetics
475 Devonshire Road Unit 100
Windsor, ON N8Y 2L5
800-465-7301 (in Canada only)
e-mail: orders@hkcanada.com

Europe: Human Kinetics
107 Bradford Road
Stanningley
Leeds LS28 6AT, United Kingdom
+44 (0) 113 255 5665
e-mail: hk@hkeurope.com

Australia: Human Kinetics
57A Price Avenue
Lower Mitcham, South Australia 5062
08 8372 0999
e-mail: liaw@hkaustralia.com

New Zealand: Human Kinetics
Division of Sports Distributors NZ Ltd.
P.O. Box 300 226 Albany
North Shore City, Auckland
0064 9 448 1207
e-mail: info@humankinetics.co.nz

Acknowledgments

I wish to thank all of the authors who worked on this project and the staff at Human Kinetics for their contributions to this book. A special thanks to my staff, coworkers, and players at Oregon State for their help in putting this book together. Thanks to my family and friends for their support and love in my journey in this sport. My new daughter Ava is the light of my life and has brought me so much joy away from the sport of softball. To Lisa F., Kelly I., Sharron B., Sue E., Dot R., Michelle G., and so many other wonderful mentors and athletes I have met, I thank you for being a part of my life and bringing me so much enjoyment in the great sport of softball.

—Kirk Walker

Contents

Drill Finder

Drill #	Drill	Offensive skills			Defensive skills			Communication	Fitness building	# of players	# of coaches	Page #
		Bunting	Hitting	Base running	Throwing	Receiving	Pitching					
						CHAPTER 1						
1	Walking Knee Hug								ST	I, SG, T	0	6
2	Walking Tin Soldier								ST	I, SG, T	0	7
3	Forward Lunge With Overhead Reach								ST	I, SG, T	0	8
4	Backward Skip With External Hip Rotation								ST	I, SG, T	0	9
5	Twisting Push-Up								ST	I, SG, T	0	10
6	High-Knee Run								A	I, SG, T	0	12
7	Scissors								A	I	0	13
8	Hopscotch								A	I	0	14
9	Ball Drop, Forward Start								A	I	1	15
10	One-Leg Hop Into Sprint								A	I, SG, T	0	16
11	Side Pass With Medicine Ball								S	I	0	17
12	Alternating Lunge and Twist With Medicine Ball								S	I	0	18
13	Russian Twist								S	I	0	19
14	Jackknife and Push-Up Combo								S	I	0	20
15	Rotator Cuff Series								S	I	0	22
16	Trap Series								S	I	0	24
17	Gold Rush								C	I, SG, T	1	26

Key *Fitness building:* C = Conditioning; F = Focus; R = Reaction; S = Strength; SP = Speed; ST = Stretching; Q = Quickness
Number of players: I = Individual; SG = Small group; T = Team

Drill #	Drill	Offensive skills			Defensive skills			Communication	Fitness building	# of players	# of coaches	Page #
		Bunting	Hitting	Base running	Throwing	Receiving	Pitching					
					CHAPTER 2							
18	Star				X	X		X	C	SG, T	0	30
19	Continuous Blocking					X			C	I	1	31
20	Down-Ups					X			C	I	0	32
21	Fly Ball Machine					X			C	I, SG	2	33
22	Range				X	X			C	I, SG	1-2	34
23	Pop Fouls and Bunts				X	X			C	I	1	35
24	Warm-Up Throwing				X	X		X	C	SG, T	0	36
25	Beat the Ball								S	SG	1-2	38
26	Continuous Fielding				X	X			C	I, SG	1	39
27	Shortstop Combo				X	X		X	C	SG	1	40
28	Second Baseman Flip				X	X			C	SG	1	41
29	Hard and Fast				X	X			C	SG	0	42
30	Take the Extra Base			X					C	SG, T	1	43
					CHAPTER 3							
31	Tennis Ball Bounce				X	X				SG, T	0	49
32	Training Paddle					X				I, SG, T	1	50
33	Fountain					X			A	SG, T	1	52
34	Throw, Run, Catch					X			C	SG, T	1	54
35	Reaction					X			R	I, SG, T	1	56
36	Popcorn					X			R	SG, T	1	57
37	Running Box				X	X			F	SG, T	0	58
38	Shoestring					X			F	SG, T	1	59
39	Barrier Catch					X				I, SG, T	1	60
40	Triangle				X	X			C	SG, T	1	61
41	Tag and Force Plays					X				I, SG	1	62

Key *Fitness building:* C = Conditioning; F = Focus; R = Reaction; S = Strength; SP = Speed; ST = Stretching; Q = Quickness
Number of players: I = Individual; SG = Small group; T = Team

Drill #	Drill	Offensive skills			Defensive skills			Communication	Fitness building	# of players	# of coaches	Page #
		Bunting	Hitting	Base running	Throwing	Receiving	Pitching					
CHAPTER 4												
42	Wrist Snaps				X					SG, T	0	65
43	Lying Wrist Snaps				X	X				I, SG, T	0	66
44	Wrist Snaps Using a Striped Ball				X	X				SG, T	0	67
45	One-Knee Throwing				X	X				SG, T	0	68
46	Bucket Throws				X					I, SG, T	1	70
47	Long-Hop Throws				X	X				SG, T	0	71
48	Front Flips				X	X			C	SG, T	0	72
49	Backhand Tosses				X	X				SG, T	0	73
50	Throwing on the Run				X	X			C	SG, T	0	74
51	Relay Throws				X	X		X	C	SG, T	0	75
52	Speed Throws				X	X			Q	SG, T	0	76
53	Four-Corner Throws				X	X		X		SG, T	0	77
54	Star Throws				X	X		X		SG, T	0	78
CHAPTER 5												
55	Plows			X					S	SG, T	0	81
56	Rubber Bands			X					S	SG, T	0	82
57	Take a Lap			X					C	I, SG, T	0	83
58	Times			X					C	I, SG, T	1	84
59	One Base			X					C	SG, T	1	85
60	Work-Up			X					C	SG, T	1	86
61	Leads and Returns			X					C	SG, T	1	87
62	4-3-2-1			X					C	SG, T	1	88
63	Clap and Go			X					C	SG, T	1	89
64	Around the Horn			X					C	SG, T	1+	90
65	Two at a Time			X				X	C	SG, T	2+	91
66	Tag-Ups			X				X	C	SG, T	2+	92

Key *Fitness building:* C = Conditioning; F = Focus; R = Reaction; S = Strength; SP = Speed; ST = Stretching; Q = Quickness
Number of players: I = Individual; SG = Small group; T = Team

Drill #	Drill	Offensive skills			Defensive skills			Communication	Fitness building	# of players	# of coaches	Page #
		Bunting	Hitting	Base running	Throwing	Receiving	Pitching					
		CHAPTER 6										
67	Dry Swings		X							I, SG	0	95
68	Mirror for Hitters		X							I, SG	1	96
69	Incline Swings		X							I, SG	0	97
70	Batting Tee		X							I, SG	0	98
71	Step Back		X							I, SG	1	99
72	Walk Through		X	X	X	X				I, SG	0	100
73	Self-Toss		X							I, SG	0	101
74	Angle Toss		X							I, SG	1	102
75	Front Toss		X							I, SG	1	103
76	Bottom Hand Extension		X							I, SG	1	104
77	Drive the Tunnel		X							I, SG	1	105
78	No Pop, No Pull		X							I, SG	1	106
79	Situational Hitting		X							I, SG	1	107
80	Stand-In		X							I, SG	0	108
81	Live Pitching, Head to Head		X							I, SG	0	109
		CHAPTER 7										
82	Shadow Bunting	X								SG, T	1	114
83	Machine Sacrifice Bunting	X								I, SG, T	1	115
84	Tee Bunts	X								I, SG, T	1	116
85	Front-Toss Bunting	X								I, SG, T	1	118
86	Location Bunting	X								I, SG, T	1	120
87	Machine Short-Game Mix	X						X		SG, T	1	121
88	Short-Game Competition	X		X	X			X		T	1-2	122
89	Game Day Squeeze Play	X		X	X			X		SG, T	1	123
90	Rapid Fire Sneaky Bunts	X								I, SG	1	124
91	Putting It All Together	X		X	X			X		T	1	125

Key *Fitness building:* C = Conditioning; F = Focus; R = Reaction; S = Strength; SP = Speed; ST = Stretching; Q = Quickness
Number of players: I = Individual; SG = Small group; T = Team

Drill #	Drill	Offensive skills			Defensive skills			Communication	Fitness building	# of players	# of coaches	Page #
		Bunting	Hitting	Base running	Throwing	Receiving	Pitching					
	CHAPTER 8											
92	Tee Work for Slappers	X								I	0	129
93	Four Corners Off the Tee	X								I	0	130
94	Horse	X								I, SG	1	131
95	Hold the Position	X								I, SG	1	132
96	Timing for Slappers	X								I, SG	1	133
97	Knock Out	X								SG	1	134
98	Bounce	X								I	1	135
99	High–Low	X								I	1	136
100	Bat Stop	X								I	1	137
101	Mirror for Slappers	X								I	1	138
	CHAPTER 9											
102	Side to Side					X			C	SG, T	1	143
103	Short Hops					X			C	SG, T	0	144
104	Run-Throughs					X			A	SG, T	1	145
105	Receiving Balls at First Base					X			A	I, SG	1	146
106	Hot Box				X	X			A	I, SG	2	147
107	Ready Position and First Step					X				I, SG	1	148
108	Five-Ball Fungo				X	X				I, SG	1	149
109	Tennis Ball Circle					X				SG	1	150
110	Infield Box				X	X				SG, T	0	152
111	Double T				X	X				I, SG	1	154
	CHAPTER 10											
112	Sideline to Sideline				X	X				SG, T	1	159
113	Loop					X				SG, T	2	160

Key *Fitness building:* C = Conditioning; F = Focus; R = Reaction; S = Strength; SP = Speed; ST = Stretching; Q = Quickness
Number of players: I = Individual; SG = Small group; T = Team

Drill #	Drill	Offensive skills			Defensive skills			Communication	Fitness building	# of players	# of coaches	Page #
		Bunting	Hitting	Base running	Throwing	Receiving	Pitching					
		CHAPTER 10 *(CONTINUED)*										
114	Zig Zag				X	X				SG, T	1	161
115	T				X	X				SG, T	1	162
116	Around the Cones				X	X				SG	1	163
117	Balls in Between				X	X				SG, T	1	164
118	Backup				X	X				T	1	165
119	Only Line of Defense				X	X				SG	0	166
120	At the Fence				X	X				SG	1	167
121	Fielding Three Ways				X	X				I, SG	1	168
122	Off the Fence				X	X				SG, T	1	169
		CHAPTER 11										
123	Resistance						X		S	I	0	173
124	One Knee						X			I	0	174
125	Slingshot Release						X			I	0	176
126	Standing Crane						X			I	0	178
127	Standing Sideways Feet Together						X			I	0	180
128	Stride Progressions						X			I	0	182
129	Swinging Crane						X			I	0	184
130	Walk-Throughs						X			I	0	186
131	Long Toss						X			I	0	187
132	Box Resistance						X			I	0	188
133	Drag Obstacle Kick						X			I	0	189
134	Football Toss						X			I	0	190
135	Target Toss						X			I	0	191
136	Tee String						X			I	0	192

Key *Fitness building:* C = Conditioning; F = Focus; R = Reaction; S = Strength; SP = Speed; ST = Stretching; Q = Quickness
Number of players: I = Individual; SG = Small group; T = Team

Drill #	Drill	Offensive skills			Defensive skills			Communication	Fitness building	# of players	# of coaches	Page #
		Bunting	Hitting	Base running	Throwing	Receiving	Pitching					
CHAPTER 12												
137	Progression Blocking					X				I	1	195
138	Three-Ball Blocking					X				I	1	196
139	Play at the Plate					X				I, SG	2	197
140	Get Up and Go Bunting				X				A	I	1	198
141	Bunting Line Drill				X					I	0	199
142	Transition				X	X				I	1	200
143	Target on the Run				X	X				I, SG	0	201
144	Pop Flies are Easy					X				I	1	202
145	Wild-Pitch Outs				X					I, SG	0	203
146	Glove to Glove				X	X			Q	I, SG	1	204
147	Split-Field Throws				X	X				I, SG	2	205
148	Shuttle Touches								C	I, SG	0	206
CHAPTER 13												
149	Six Pitch		X							I	1	211
150	Major League		X							I, SG	1	212
151	Focused Batting Practice	X	X	X				X		I, SG, T	1	213
152	Point Game	X	X	X	X	X		X		SG, T	1	214
153	Consequences	X	X	X	X	X		X		SG, T	1	215
154	Short Game	X		X						SG, T	1	216
155	Runners in Motion	X	X	X						SG, T	1	217
156	Pressure Bunt	X		X						SG, T	1	218
157	Isolation Offense			X				X		SG	0	219
158	RBI		X	X						SG	0	220
159	Twenty-One	X	X	X				X		SG, T	2+	221

Key *Fitness building:* C = Conditioning; F = Focus; R = Reaction; S = Strength; SP = Speed; ST = Stretching; Q = Quickness
Number of players: I = Individual; SG = Small group; T = Team

Drill #	Drill	Offensive skills			Defensive skills			Communication	Fitness building	# of players	# of coaches	Page #
		Bunting	Hitting	Base running	Throwing	Receiving	Pitching					
	CHAPTER 13 *(CONTINUED)*											
160	Softball Yahtzee	X	X	X				X		SG, T	1	222
161	Short-Game Reads	X		X				X		SG, T	0	224
162	Hit and Run, Run, Run		X	X						SG, T	0	225
163	Ducks on the Pond	X	X	X				X		SG, T	1	226
164	First-and-Third Offensive Options			X				X		SG, T	1	228
	CHAPTER 14											
165	21 in a Row				X	X		X		T	1	231
166	ABCs of First and Third				X	X		X		SG, T	1	232
167	Infield/Outfield Together Rounds				X	X		X		T	1	234
168	Two-Man Infield Fungo				X	X		X		SG, T	2	236
169	Pop-Up/Shallow Fly Ball				X	X		X		SG, T	2	237
170	Defending the Short Game				X	X		X		SG, T	0	238
171	Rundowns			X	X	X		X		SG, T	0	239
172	Outfield Shallow Relay or Cutoff			X	X	X		X		SG, T	1	240
173	Defensive Scouting Report				X	X		X		SG, T	1	242
174	Prime Time Defense			X	X	X		X		T	1	243
175	Deep Relays and Cutoffs			X	X	X		X		T	1	244
176	Four Points					X		X		SG, T	1	247
177	Right Side–Left Side Cross Fire					X				SG, T	2	248

Key *Fitness building:* C = Conditioning; F = Focus; R = Reaction; S = Strength; SP = Speed; ST = Stretching; Q = Quickness
Number of players: I = Individual; SG = Small group; T = Team

Preface

From beginning to advanced levels of play, all softball players and coaches need drills to practice the game. As coaches, the contributors of this book have spent the majority of their professional and playing careers training to be successful, and they have all found favorite drills that they wish to share with you. Young or old, rookie or veteran, every softball player can use the drills in these chapters to better her game. I encourage every reader to enter into a search for knowledge and insight with the pages that follow.

Each chapter was written by a successful Division I coach with great passion for the game and includes the drills that they use either in their programs on a daily basis, or during their camps, clinics, and preseason development sessions. I have also added to these chapters many of my favorite drills. The catching, throwing, bunting, team offense, and team defense chapters all include several drills that I have used during my time at UCLA, Oregon State, and with the USA National Team. In addition to the drills, each coach has written a short introduction explaining the importance of the chapter's area of focus. I encourage you to read these prior to looking at the drills in order to gain some insight into the philosophy and approach of that coach. Finally, there is a short biography of each contributor in the back of the book that describes where each coach gained his or her tremendous experience.

Each chapter of this book focuses on a specific skill or attribute needed to be successful at every level of softball. Part I includes chapters on warming up and conditioning. Part II covers the basics of catching, throwing, base running, hitting, bunting, and slapping, which are the fundamental skills and building blocks of softball. Part III includes position-specific drills for the infielder, outfielder, pitcher, and catcher. Finally, part IV includes team offense and team defense drills that will help the coach or team master these aspects of the game.

Each chapter includes 10 to 14 drills that will help athletes at all levels. Each drill should be read fully before execution in order to explore the intensity level. If the drill appears to be too easy or fundamental for your needed level, you may find that the variation section provides a way to alter the drill to fit your needs. Also be sure to read the coaching points section of each drill, as it is one of the greatest sources of information specific to the actual drill.

Drills are categorized in a number of different ways in the drill finder on pages vi to xiii to enable coaches and players to reference drills that cross over to other areas. For example, many drills throughout the book can be used for conditioning even though they are not found in the conditioning chapter. There are also a number of drills across the chapters that focus on throwing or receiving, or even communication. I encourage you to fully explore the drill finder and take advantage of the crossover from chapter to chapter.

This book has been a labor of love about the sport of softball and the skills it takes to be successful. I have thoroughly enjoyed serving as the editor for this book. I hand selected each of the contributors not only because they are successful coaches, but mostly because they are tremendous people who have great passion for the sport and the athletes that play for them. In coordinating the chapters and overseeing the entire content, I have gained even more respect for these coaches. I know that in using this drill book you will discover that regardless of your level of play, you can have great passion for this sport while learning something new every day.

Enjoy your journey through this book and through your experience in softball. Always cherish the time you get to spend playing or coaching the greatest game ever invented. Always be willing to share your knowledge with others, just as the coaches and contributors in this book have committed to do. We are stewards of this sport, and none of us own the sport or the knowledge we gain. It is our job to help better our teammates, our coaches, and yes, even our competitors. If you can help your competitors be better, the level of our sport will grow to new heights, and our love for the game will be multiplied. Softball is a great game, but only a game. When the last out is made and the game is over, never forget that the joy of the game comes from playing and competing and not from winning the game alone.

—Kirk Walker, Editor

Key to Diagrams

△   Cone

⟶   Player movement

┄┄➤   Throw

┅┅➤   Ground ball

╌╌➤   Hit

CO   Coach

X   Player

C   Catcher

P   Pitcher

1B   First baseman

2B   Second baseman

3B   Third baseman

SS   Shortstop

RF   Right fielder

CF   Centerfielder

LF   Left fielder

R   Runner

B   Batter

Ⓜ   Ball machine

Using Drills Effectively

Kirk Walker *Oregon State University Head Coach*

In this book we'll take a look at how some of the most successful collegiate programs in the country use drills to practice the sport of fastpitch softball. A drill can be defined as the isolation of a physical or technical skill outside of the environment of an actual game. The key word here is *isolation* because it is often by separating or isolating a skill from its usual context that we can best teach our players the full value of the skill and how to improve in executing it. Yes, players might improve in, say, throwing ability by throwing a lot of balls in practice within the context of gamelike competition or casual games of catch with teammates. But if we want them to fully understand and appreciate the factors that determine whether a throw reaches its target at the precise angle, position, speed, and time that we desire, we need to isolate the skill, break it down into its parts, and then work on each of those parts before building the skill back up to whole again. This is where drills come in very handy.

The sport of fastpitch softball can be easily broken down into parts, the most obvious of which are offense and defense. Everything that we know about our sport falls into either an offensive or defensive category. If we look at these two areas of our game, we find a number of smaller components that can be isolated and thus more easily taught. On the offensive side, these include hitting, bunting, base running, slapping, and creating offensive strategies. On the defensive side, they include throwing, receiving, infield play, outfield play, pitching, catching, and defensive strategies.

Each of these components deserves its own chapter, which is exactly what we are pleased to provide in this book. Each chapter has been written by a coach at one of the best collegiate programs in the country. We have also included chapters on conditioning drills and drills that players and teams can use to warm up before games or practices. Each chapter contains detailed instructions for drills used to isolate skills that our players must master if they are to be fully effective during games. Drills range in focus from the most basic of skills for beginning players to the most advanced skills for players in collegiate programs around the country.

The Value of Drills

During my 22 years of coaching division I softball, one thing that has become overwhelmingly obvious is the value of using drills in practice. One value of drills is their ability to incorporate a high level of repetitions within a short amount of time. Coaches must use drills in practice to make the best use of their limited time with their players. Drills ensure that every essential component of the sport can receive its time in practice. Anything that can happen in a game can be drilled in a practice. Obviously, some skills, such as pitching and hitting, are essential in every inning of every game. Other skills, such as putting down a bunt, are used only a few times over the course of a game. Still other skills, such as the suicide squeeze, might come into play in only a few games all season. But no matter how rarely a skill is needed, we never know for sure when we're going to need it. This is why every player on every squad must be ready for every possible situation on every night. How can this happen? How can a coach balance practice time to cover all the possible situations and skills needed? Drills, drills, and more drills!

Good drills help coaches and players prepare for the season. Another value of good drills is that they can evolve and progress as the skill levels of your players progress. A final value for some drills comes when players are able to get feedback on proper mechanics. These types of drills are not just about repetition—they isolate and reinforce proper technique.

Drills that stand the test of time are those that can accomplish three objectives. First, the drill must give players an opportunity to practice a specific skill with repetition. Make sure the drills you choose give your players repetitions of skills they'll need in a game. Practicing any drill that doesn't have a specific purpose might help with conditioning but won't help a player get better at a specific skill. Always look for drills that focus on functional skill development.

Second, a good drill should give a player a clear and simple goal to accomplish. It should be easy for players to measure their success. Many players approach drill work as a waste of time as they want to actually hit or play a real game. If players are given clear goals for drills and understand how the drills will help them be better softball players, they'll be more focused and committed. Coaches should attempt to execute drills themselves before asking their players to attempt them. This can and should actually be done outside or away from practice to ensure that a drill is safe, appropriate, and beneficial in helping players learn the specific goal of the drill. Attempting these drills away from the players helps the coach fully understand and relate to the struggles or challenges that are created in a particular drill. Trial runs will also be helpful to coaches if they are going to demonstrate or show the drill to their players during practice.

Third, a drill should be able to apply to all skill levels of players. The sport of softball is a simple one with basic building blocks needed for success. Players at all levels need to be able to execute these fundamentals correctly and efficiently. If a drill doesn't apply to skills that even the best players need to do, then it might not have a use in practice. Although many of our elite players have already mastered some of the basic skills, a drill should still be appropriate to the proper execution of the skill by all levels of players.

If a drill meets these three criteria, it will be a valuable tool for as long as you coach. Having a large arsenal of drills to choose from will help you reach a greater variety of players during your career. Every player learns the game at her own pace, and drills help to make sure that all the players on your team are given the best opportunity to learn. As you know, softball players have diverse learning styles. This being the case, we need a variety of drills to reach all of our players in different ways. Whether your players are visual learners, auditory learners, or kinesthetic learners, each drill should have value that different players can derive in different ways.

The great thing about drills is that they can always be altered or adapted to the level of the player being taught. If you have ever run into frustration when teaching an athletic skill to a player, you know how important it is to be able to explain and break down skills. Drills help coaches give their players experience and repetition without wasting a lot of valuable practice time.

One final value of drills is their benefit in providing body awareness or kinesthetic information. Knowing where your body is in space and how your body moves is the key to any athletic movement. Drills give players feedback about their body awareness, which can improve their ability to make changes. If a player can feel what she is doing wrong, she can make some body changes that feel different to her. Once a player can feel what it takes to execute a skill correctly, a drill becomes the vehicle for repetition and muscle memory. Once a player reaches that point when she can successfully repeat the drill correctly because of good muscle memory, it's time to make some adjustments to that drill to add another level of challenge.

How to Create Your Own Drills

Using drills as teaching tools is the most effective way to educate and train players. In this book you'll find drills from some of the best collegiate programs in the country. These coaches have years of experience and a wealth of knowledge they're willing to share. Some of their favorite drills are provided here. Many of these drills have been passed on for generations. Some have been altered or revised as the understanding of the game has changed. In addition to those drills that have passed the test of time, there are always new drills being created. Many coaches have learned the art of creating drills or inventing new ways to teach skills. It's no surprise that variation on drills occurs with frequency from coach to coach.

Let's look at the five steps to creating drills of your own.

1. Define and isolate a specific skill. To create your own drill you must first think about specific skills of the sport and isolate them from the rest of the game. Looking at a small component of athletic movement will give you those skills. If you're not sure if something is a valuable skill or not, just take a look at what the best and most successful players in our sport do well. Isolating specific skills with drills can be a great learning tool for players as well as for coaches to explain the great game of softball.

2. Define proper mechanics and technique for that skill. Once you have isolated a specific skill to work on, you need to think about the proper mechanics needed to execute that skill successfully. For example, how do the infielders on the United States Olympic team or a top collegiate program throw to first base? How do the top collegiate players effectively advance runners with their bunting technique? If you're going to ask developing players to do something with specific mechanics, make sure that those mechanics are really what need to happen. Many times we teach only what we were taught without really understanding why. I often challenge coaches to be able to explain and justify why a certain skill should be executed in a certain way. Being able to show supportive information with demonstration or video footage can be a powerful teaching tool.

3. Establish steps to execute repetition of proper technique. Use your knowledge of the mechanics you have isolated and investigated to set clear and defined steps that will reinforce the proper goal or technique that you want your players to learn. To do this, take advantage of many different methods, including using tools from outside our game: tennis balls, Wiffle balls, small bats, cones, paddles—anything that can help you get your point across to your players. Some drills can be done in a variety of ways while still focusing on the primary mechanics. These variations should be viewed as ways to help players become kinesthetically aware of their bodies. Playing without a glove, using a smaller ball, swinging a heavier bat, and so on can sometimes make a player focus differently or possibly feel the skill in a way that makes sense to her.

4. Put safety first. A critically important principle in creating, altering, or developing drills is to make sure the drill is safe for your players and for the coaches involved. Taking the time to attempt the drill yourself might prevent many injuries or needless problems. Never put your players in a position to be injured or hurt because of the setup of a drill. For example, if you're going to ask a player to gain resistance by hitting a basketball off a tee, make sure the basketball is deflated so the rebound of the bat off the basketball doesn't strike your hitter in the nose at full force. Surprisingly, many players and coaches have been hurt because a drill was not considered in terms of safety. Coaches should never ask their players to do something that they haven't done and aren't willing to do themselves.

5. Clearly define goals for proper execution. Clearly defined goals for a drill will help every player in her execution and motivation. Clarity can be accomplished verbally or visually, or sometimes via some other measure of success within the drill. For example, if the goal of the drill is accuracy, then having clearly defined measures of accuracy will help players achieve success. Competition can be an element within nearly any drill. Players are by nature competitive in sport, so using competition against their own previous score or their teammates can sometimes be effective for increased motivation. But be careful about using competition for every drill. Players sometimes need to feel pure reward for just executing a skill correctly. Today's players are sometimes not given the opportunity to take pride in doing something well without getting something in return.

Variations on any drill are important so that coaches can more easily suit the elements of the drill to their particular players. Using variations within a drill can also help with visual focus or body awareness. For example, drills done with regular size balls can often be done with smaller balls, tennis balls, or small Wiffle balls. Having players do some drills with no gloves or with paddles can change the complexity of the drill. Remember that safety should always be considered with every variation as well. Coaches should have a good understanding of their players and their confidence levels. Sometimes coaches will need to mix in variations of the drills so that they will ensure success for the players. Other times using variations to challenge them and give them more failure might be an important component. Players should learn more from their failures than their successes if given the proper feedback. Success and failure are both important experiences for players to be able to grow in their ability.

Here is a simple example of applying the necessary steps a coach goes through in creating or developing a drill:

Step 1: A coach wants to help his outfielders with their first steps on a fly ball. First, reduce the number of options that your players need to consider. You can do this by designating the shoulder and direction of the fly ball you're going to simulate. This is the first step: isolating the skill.

Step 2: Inform the player of the proper technique that you want them to accomplish. For example, you might show them how to use a weight shift or a drop step. This is the second step: defining proper mechanics or technique.

Step 3: Start the drill by throwing and not hitting a fly ball, thus controlling that variable. This is the third step: establishing steps for proper execution and repetition.

Step 4: Make sure there are no obstacles that players will run into and that the sun won't be glaring in their eyes (unless that's part of the drill). This is the fourth step: safety first.

Step 5: Explain what you're hoping your players will accomplish; in this example it's footwork. Keep the focus on the goal and not on peripheral issues, such as making the catch. This is the fifth step: clearly define goals for proper execution.

Using Drills in Practices

Several questions commonly come up when considering how to use drills in practice. How much time in practice should be spent on drills? How should drills be incorporated into practice? Do I change my drill work as the season moves on? Let's look at a few principles of learning as we try to unravel these questions.

First, new skills are best learned when they're done in the least stressful and most repetitive fashion. You might have heard the term *block learning*. The easiest way to describe block learning is that you take a single isolated skill or movement and focus on *only* that skill. Eliminating the challenge of decision making or subsequent skill execution helps the learning process in the beginning. Giving your players instruction and feedback for proper muscle memory becomes important. Most of your block learning should occur in the off-season or far away from the start of your actual season. This is the best time to break down skills into smaller, more manageable parts. This is also the best time to make major changes to a player's technique. Muscle memory of the correct movement is the goal. If you can get a player to feel the correct movement over and over, you will likely create a muscle pattern that she can call on later during stressful pressure situations in games.

Using isolated drills in block format is the best way to accomplish this. Drills that focus on the most minute and specific movements are best. These are often thought of as fundamental drills. The more these drills are done, the more competent your players should become, which eventually allows you to spend less time on the drills. Many fundamental drills should be done throughout the season, but the amount of time spent on them is drastically reduced by late in the season.

As practices progress, so should many of the drills. Teaching in stages helps build trust in players. Drills that focus on larger movements or full execution can now be introduced. These generally include more adjustments or decision-making processes during the execution. Block learning is still a good method because repetition allows for the greatest amount of feedback. Feedback comes from the coaches, failure of the skill, and, one hopes, proper execution of the drill.

A player must trust the proper execution of the skill before she'll ever be able to consistently execute under pressure. Gamelike drills with added pressure are not done at every practice but can be used to create variety in practices. Skill drills are primarily individual in nature and still don't require a lot more than one play to interact. These skill-development drills really become a coach's guide on when players are ready to move on to more demanding pressure-type drills. Early on you might see a lot of inconsistency with these types of drills. Players might look great one day and horrible the next. This is generally because these are drills that require more than just muscle memory. The more the drills are done over time, the more consistency will develop.

As players' skills develop further you can start to introduce drills that are more interactive. These are drills that apply to a segment of the game rather than to just one physical skill. These types of drills will incorporate communication between players, require multiple player involvement, or focus on a specific game situation (e.g., field bunts, double plays, relays). It's still a good idea to work on these drills or skills in block segments in the beginning. For example, make sure that you spend time working on fielding balls and throwing to first base before you require a player to try to throw out an actual runner running down the line. Similarly, work on double-play footwork repetitions before your players have to read runners and full infield situations.

Finally, your drill work in practice can simulate more gamelike or random situations. These types of drills can still isolate situations, but there is more than one option for execution. Offensively, this is analogous to batting in gamelike drills off of live pitching. This is the last form of learning that requires gamelike judgment or more random decision making during the execution of skills. Your players might not be doing the exact same skill in repetition because there are other variables or options. Some drills can simulate this, as you'll see in the chapters ahead.

Based on this timeline, most of your practices early on will be almost exclusively drills. Early on those drills will be primarily skill development. Later in your season, you'll still want to figure how to incorporate drill work into a practice scheme. Many great programs use a short segment at the beginning of every practice for fundamental warm-up skills. These are a set of drills that your players will do every day before practice, although the number of reps might be drastically reduced over time. For example, early in the season players might need 10 to 15 reps of a drill to fine tune them. By later in the season and after doing these drills daily, players might need only 3 to 5 reps to reinforce the skill and warm up. Generally, coaches keep these daily fundamentals to 15 to 20 minutes at the beginning of practice.

Determining Which Drills to Use

Coaches are faced with the challenge of trying to isolate a specific skill and help players master that skill. You can never have enough drills in your coaching arsenal. Pick up new drills or variations on drills whenever you can. Many variations on drills come from different sports. Athletic movement is similar across many sports. The more prepared you are to help your players, the better coach you're able to be. I believe true coaches are always learning and expanding their scope of knowledge. Some coaches become complacent or comfortable with how they teach a skill or run a practice. The great coaches are constantly seeking better ways to explain the same skills they have taught. They also seek ways to practice this great game of softball differently to keep players challenged and motivated.

Yes, you are always to be seeking out new and innovative drills, but there are some drills that will remain a part of your teaching arsenal for your entire coaching career. These effective drills might have been taught to you as a player or learned very early in your career. Some of these you might find in the upcoming chapters. If you do, I encourage you to explore the variations that these great coaches might have added to the drills. One of the greatest things about drills is you can never have enough, and you can always improve on them. Some teaching techniques or mechanics have changed over the years, which means the drills we use to reinforce or teach these mechanics might have also changed.

Many collegiate programs have proven success in the teaching of softball skills. The chapters that follow will give you a snapshot of some of the great teachers in our game. I have personally chosen the programs and coaches in this book because of the great amount of respect I have for them. There are many other programs and coaches that I respect highly, but I do think that the ones highlighted here have much to offer anyone wanting to gain knowledge. A goal in creating this book is to provide an ongoing reference manual for coaches to use daily throughout their careers.

The format of the chapters and each drill is set up to give coaches everything they need to know when setting up and using each drill. There are sections that describe the equipment needed, setup required, details of the drill, variations of the drills, purpose of the drills, and additional teaching or coaching points. Give yourself and your players the opportunity to use the same drills that thousands of collegiate players have learned from to become All Americans, National Champions, Olympians, or simply better softball players. Regardless of the skill level of your players, there is invaluable information in the upcoming pages that will benefit this great sport of softball and the players who play it every day.

Training Drills

Chapter 1

Warming Up

Carol Bruggeman   *University of Louisville Associate Head Coach*

Teena Murray   *University of Louisville*
Director of Olympic Sports Performance

Softball players love to hit, throw, pitch, make great defensive plays, and score lots of runs. It's exciting and exhilarating to rip a double, make a diving catch for a crucial out, or make that perfect pitch on the corner of the plate for a strikeout. Ask any softball player what she enjoys most about the game of softball, and she'll most likely name a particular skill such as hitting or an aspect such as the heat of competition. One area she probably won't mention is warming up before a game or practice. Many players view the warm-up as a boring activity they must endure in order to play. Still, if pressed, most players will concede the importance of a proper warm-up.

Skipping a full warm-up should never be an option. If your players fail to warm up properly, the quality of their game will be affected, and they'll increase their risk of injury. All coaches and players must understand the benefits of a productive, softball-specific warm-up. Performed properly, the warm-up can be as valuable to a team as a timely pinch hit or a double play. Simply put, an effective warm-up is essential for preparing players for competition.

Players and coaches need to understand the necessary athletic skills and softball-specific movement patterns required to play the game of softball. Before designing your warm-up drills, you need a baseline knowledge of *how* softball players move on the field and *why* they move that way. Athleticism is movement, and preparing or warming up softball players to move more efficiently, effectively, and explosively requires an examination of the game. Both on offense and defense, the critical aspects of movement include acceleration speed and multidirectional quickness.

The human body moves in three planes: sagittal, frontal, and transverse. In softball, efficient, effective, and explosive movement is required in all three planes.

- **Sagittal (forward and backward):** This plane is dominant in base running and in some fielding and throwing.
- **Frontal (side to side):** This is the least important plane in softball but is sometimes used in fielding and is important in training for injury prevention.
- **Transverse (rotation):** This is the most important plane of motion in softball and is used extensively for pitching, throwing, hitting, and fielding. Power in the transverse plane is critical for generating bat speed and balance in all softball skills. Coordination in this plane permits solid bat contact.

Softball is a power game. Every action in the game is explosive in nature. In fact, most actions on the field take three seconds or less. With this in mind, players should perform dynamic warm-up routines that include movements in all three planes; such a warm-up prepares the body to execute the actions of softball safely and effectively. During the warm-up, both the central nervous system and the musculoskeletal system (muscles, tendons, ligaments) must be properly prepared.

Four areas critical to address when creating effective warm-up drills for softball are mobility; speed, agility, and quickness; core strength; and shoulder prehab.

Drills 1 through 6 in this chapter are designed to develop mobility, which refers to efficient and controlled movement. Efficient mobility requires perfect posture, stability, coordination, and flexibility through large ranges of motion, beginning with simple, low-tempo movements and advancing to more complex, high-tempo movements. Many softball players struggle to perform simple movements such as skipping, bending, and lunging, without losing their balance and resorting to poor posture. On the other hand, mobile softball players can move their bodies with strength and stability while performing a wide range of dynamic movements. These players are generally able to perform softball skills at higher levels with a reduced risk of injury.

Mobility can be significantly improved through targeted warm-ups. Help players to remember that posture, balance, and rhythm are their goals while warming up. Players should spend 10 to 15 minutes on the mobility segment of the warm-up. This will increase core temperature, increase blood flow, lubricate joints, warm muscles, challenge dynamic flexibility and balance, improve coordination, reduce the risk of injury, and stimulate the nervous system, which increases awareness and alertness.

Drills 7 through 10 are designed to develop speed, agility, and quickness. These three words, although often used interchangeably, in fact refer to separate aspects of softball performance that must be developed through training and warm-up routines. Although softball players rarely hit top speed, softball is a speed game! The speed that's essential for a game-changing performance in softball is not top-end speed but acceleration speed, which is defined as the rate of change of speed. In other words, how quickly can players get their body started and generate significant speed? Acceleration speed relies heavily on leg power and stride frequency. Learning to be more efficient and effective with the first one to four steps is the primary aim of acceleration training. Including a few short sprints at the end of the warm-up session prepares the body to move at game speed.

Agility is the ability to change directions quickly. Some might argue that agility is equally as important as speed and quickness, but there are very few situations in a softball game in which a player is required to change directions. Thus, the majority of warm-up routines should focus on speed and quickness.

Quickness refers to reaction time and the first step, both critical aspects of the game of softball. How quickly can a defensive player react to the ball coming at her and move to field it? How quickly can a hitter react to bat contact and get that critical first step toward first base? Quickness depends on concentration (or awareness) and anticipation. To be effective, quickness warm-up drills should emphasize proper footwork, reacting to a stimulus, and competition. Drills should be conducted over short distances, and players should get complete rest between sets. Speed and quickness warm-up drills should never feel like conditioning.

Drills 11 through 14 are designed to build core strength. The body is a linked system that works together to produce movement. The most important section of this linked system is the core. This is the body's center of gravity, the area where all movements are initiated and through which all forces are transferred. Core musculature includes the upper and lower abdominals, obliques, lower back, and the hips. The functional strength of the core determines the effectiveness of softball movements—from running, jumping, throwing, swinging the bat, pitching, and fielding.

Core muscles permit flexion and extension of the trunk, lateral flexion, and rotation. Most important, they play a critical role in the stabilization of the spine during movement and the transfer of force from the core to the bat. Core exercises should be included in a softball warm-up and should include movements similar to those performed on the field.

Drills 15 and 16 are for shoulder prehab. Shoulder injuries are the most common injury in softball, with impingement and instability injuries leading the way. The most common causes of shoulder injuries—poor posture, repetitive trauma (often from poor mechanics), and overtraining—are preventable. Special attention needs to be given to strengthening the muscles around the shoulder joint (the rotator cuff and scapular area) during training and warm-ups to prevent these types of injuries.

Although time frames will vary, at least 15 to 20 minutes is necessary for an effective softball warm-up. If the essential ingredients as previously described are incorporated into your softball practice and competition warm-up routines, your team will be well prepared and ready to perform at a high level. Helping your team understand and appreciate the importance of a softball-specific, dynamic warm-up is a critical step in preparing them for success on the softball diamond.

WALKING KNEE HUG

Purpose

To warm up the lower body and back

Organization

Players position on the outfield foul line in rows of three, with at least 5 yards (4.5 meters) between players. This drill should be performed for 20 yards (18 meters). Once the first player finishes her 20 yards, the next player in line begins the drill.

Execution

Players interlock fingers, cup the knee with the fingers, and pull the knee to the chest, keeping the back straight, head up, and eyes forward. They drive up onto the toe of the supporting leg and press the hips forward. Alternate legs and repeat.

Variation

Add skipping to the drill.

Coaching Points

Make sure players use full range of motion and pull knees tightly to chest.

Purpose
To warm up the hamstrings

Organization
Players position on the outfield foul line in rows of three, with at least 5 yards (4.5 meters) between players. This drill should be performed for 20 yards (18 meters). Once the first player finishes her 20 yards, the next player in line begins the drill.

Execution
Holding hands at eye level, players walk forward, kicking right leg to right hand and left leg to left hand, alternating legs. The head stays up with eyes forward and back straight.

Variation
Add skipping to the drill.

Coaching Points
To stretch their hamstrings, players should keep their arms at eye level and bring their legs to their hands, not the other way around.

3   FORWARD LUNGE WITH OVERHEAD REACH

Purpose
To warm up the hip flexors, quads, and core

Organization
Players position on the outfield foul line in rows of three, with at least 5 yards (4.5 meters) between players. This drill should be performed for 20 yards (18 meters). Once the first player finishes her 20 yards, the next player in line begins the drill.

Execution
Players take a long stride forward with the right leg and lower their hips to the ground by bending the knees. The upper body remains straight. As the back knee is lowered toward the ground, the front knee should be bent at a 90-degree angle. Players return to standing and bring feet together between each alternating stride.

Variations
To add an upper body stretch, have players interlock their fingers with palms facing away and push palms away from the body. With each stride, they reach above their head and reach back behind the body as far as they can go. Add a reverse lunge or lateral lunge to warm up additional muscles.

Coaching Points
Make sure players use a full range of motion with long strides and fully extended arms. Do not rush this drill.

4 BACKWARD SKIP WITH EXTERNAL HIP ROTATION

Purpose

To warm up the lower body and hip rotators

Organization

Players position on the outfield foul line in rows of three, with at least 5 yards (4.5 meters) between players. This drill should be performed for 20 yards (18 meters). Once the first player finishes her 20 yards, the next player in line begins the drill.

Execution

Players pull their heels to their hamstrings, then open up the hip 90 degrees and step back while pushing off the ground with the supporting leg in a skipping motion. Players should focus on maximizing external rotation of the hip to stretch the groin area.

Variation

Increase the pace to increase heart rate.

Coaching Points

Make sure players use a full range of motion to maximize the stretch.

5   TWISTING PUSH-UP

Purpose
To warm up the upper body, core, pecs, and anterior delts

Organization
Players position on the outfield foul line in rows of three, with at least 5 yards (4.5 meters) between players.

Execution
Players perform a good push-up *(a)*; at the top of the movement, they lift the left hand off the ground and open the hips and shoulders to 90 degrees while balancing on one arm *(b)*. This brings a good stretch in the chest and shoulders. Repeat using the right side. Players should do 5 reps per side for a total of 10.

Variation
For an additional challenge, have players position their feet on an elevated surface, such as a bench.

Coaching Points
Opening the hips and shoulders to 90 degrees might be a challenge initially. Have players open up as far as is comfortable (maybe 45 degrees) until they're confident with this drill.

Purpose

To warm up the whole body

Organization

Players position on the outfield foul line in rows of three, with at least 5 yards (4.5 meters) between players. This drill should be performed for 20 yards (18 meters). Once the first player finishes her 20 yards, the next player in line begins the drill.

Execution

Players run forward while maintaining good upright posture. The lower back remains tight, with chest out, head up, and eyes forward. On each stride, players bring a knee up so that the heel clears the top of the opposite knee. They should coordinate arms so that the left arm is forward as the right knee comes up.

Variation

Vary the length of the stride.

Coaching Points

Make sure players keep their shoulders and entire body relaxed. Emphasize arm action.

7   SCISSORS

Purpose
To warm up footwork

Organization
Place an agility ladder (or tape on the ground or lines in the dirt) on the outfield grass or infield surface. If you have only one ladder, all players should be in a single-file line behind the ladder. If you have multiple ladders, divide the team up evenly behind each ladder.

Execution
Players begin facing the side of the ladder. They jump forward into the first box, splitting their legs so that the right leg is in while the left leg is out (*a*). They then jump again, switching positions with their legs so that the left leg is in and the right leg is out of the same box (*b*). They should continue in this fashion, moving as quickly as they can.

Variations
Move two boxes at a time instead of one. If two ladders are available, make each rep a competition between players.

Coaching Points
Make sure proper arm action is included in the warm-up.

HOPSCOTCH

Purpose
To warm up footwork

Organization
Place an agility ladder (or tape on the ground or lines in the dirt) on the outfield grass or infield surface. If you have only one ladder, all players should be in a single-file line behind the ladder. If you use multiple ladders, divide the team up evenly behind each ladder.

Execution
Players start facing the end of the ladder and straddling the first box *(a)*. They jump and quickly bring both feet together into the first box *(b)*. They jump again and land straddling the second box. Players move up the ladder as quickly as they can, staying on the balls of their feet.

Variations
To increase difficulty, place the ladder on a moderate downhill grade. If two ladders are available, make each rep a competition between players.

Coaching Points
Watch for players moving their feet quickly. They shouldn't be touching the ground for very long.

BALL DROP, FORWARD START

Purpose
To warm up footwork

Organization
Standing five yards (4.5 meters) in front of a player, a coach holds a ball in an outstretched arm at chest high. The player is in a running position with either leg forward.

Execution
Players work on reaction time, first-step quickness, and acceleration mechanics. As soon as the ball is released, the player explodes out of her starting position with a short but powerful first step. She tries to catch the ball after only one bounce.

Variations
Increase the distance between the player and coach. Try a side start instead of a front start position. Make this drill a competition between two players: Who can catch the ball first?

Coaching Points
Make sure the first few steps are short and explosive; emphasize turning the feet over quickly.

ONE-LEG HOP INTO SPRINT

Purpose
To warm up footwork

Organization
Players position on the outfield foul line in rows of three, with at least 5 yards (4.5 meters) between players. This drill should be performed for 20 yards (18 meters). Once the first player finishes her 20 yards, the next player in line begins the drill.

Execution
Standing on one leg *(a)*, players hop forward as far as they can, landing on the same leg they were standing on *(b)*. They then immediately lean, fall, and accelerate forward into a sprint for the remainder of the distance.

Variations
Run the drill with a two-leg hop instead of using one leg. Develop competitions between players.

Coaching Points
Landing the hop(s) under control is vital for success in this drill.

11   SIDE PASS WITH MEDICINE BALL

Purpose
To warm up the core

Organization
Each player needs a medicine ball and a wall or other hard surface to throw the ball against.

Execution
Standing sideways to the wall with feet shoulder-width apart, players hold the medicine ball in both hands, away from the body, with arms straight (a). They twist at the waist explosively and throw the ball forcefully at the wall (b). Have them work both sides.

Coaching Points
Make sure players are using core muscles and not only their shoulders and arms.

12 ALTERNATING LUNGE AND TWIST WITH MEDICINE BALL

Purpose
To warm up the core

Organization
Each player needs a medicine ball and approximately five yards (4.5 meters) of space.

Execution
Players hold the medicine ball in both hands with arms extended chest high (a). They lunge forward with the left leg, lower their hips toward the ground by bending their knees, and rotate 90 degrees at the waist. They then turn the head and shoulders toward the left with the ball (b). They return to neutral position and push the body back up to an upright position. Alternate legs and repeat.

Variation
Have players do a reverse lunge instead of a forward lunge.

Coaching Points
Players should keep the ball chest high and not let it drop.

13   RUSSIAN TWIST

Purpose
To warm up the core

Organization
Each player (or group of players) needs a stability ball and 10 yards (9 meters) of space.

Execution
Players lie face up on top of the ball. The ball is under the shoulder blades, knees are bent 90 degrees, and feet are flat on the ground. Arms should be extended above the chest, perpendicular to the ground, with elbows locked and palms together (a). Players rotate at the waist, twisting 90 degrees to one side as the ball is rolled to the opposite side. They attempt to twist until their arms are parallel to the ground and the ball is under the outside of the shoulder (b). They then return to neutral position and twist to the opposite side.

Variation
To increase difficulty, have players hold a medicine ball or light dumbbell.

Coaching Points
Watch for players keeping their hips up and arms straight. They should control their motions with their core muscles.

14   JACKKNIFE AND PUSH-UP COMBO

Purpose
To warm up the core

Organization
Each player (or group of players) needs a stability ball and 10 yards (9 meters) of space.

Execution
Facing the ground, players begin with the stability ball under their knees with their legs straight and hands on the floor. They bend their knees, contract their core muscles, and roll the ball forward slowly until it's directly under their chest. They then slowly roll the ball back to the starting position and do a good push-up. Core muscles remain tight throughout.

Variations
To work the external obliques more, have players roll the ball forward toward the right shoulder and then left shoulder instead of straight under the chest. Increase difficulty by starting with the ball under the toes rather than under the knees (a, b).

Coaching Points
Players need to keep their core muscles tight throughout the drill. They shouldn't sag their hips.

Purpose

To warm up the shoulders

Organization

For each of the following exercises, players hold their thumbs up for 10 reps and then down for 10 reps.

Execution

T: Raise arms to shoulder height at sides of body to make a T *(a)*.

Y: Raise arms to shoulder height at 45 degrees to form a Y *(b)*.

W: Bend forward at waist to flatten back; begin with arms straight and hanging under chest; bend elbows at 90 degrees and externally rotate shoulders, turning palms up and forward *(c)*.

Variation

Players hold a 2.5-pound (1.1-kilogram) plate in each hand. Add two reps every one to two weeks.

Coaching Points

Remind players to focus on using the shoulder muscles to perform each exercise.

Purpose
To warm up the shoulders

Organization
For each of the following exercises, players do 10 reps while holding a 2.5-pound (1.1-kilogram) plate in each hand.

Execution
Shrugs: Begin with arms relaxed and hanging at sides; shrug shoulders, elevating shoulders to ears (a).

Scap row: Bend forward at waist to flatten back; begin with arms straight and shoulders relaxed (b); without bending elbows, retract shoulder blades and hold for two seconds (c).

Scap push-up: Begin in push-up position with arms straight and elbows locked (d); keeping arms straight, retract shoulder blades (e) and then return to starting position and repeat. Hips stay up and core muscles stay tight throughout the exercise.

Variations
Have players perform the scap row with an elastic cord. Have them do the scap push-up on an unstable surface, such as a medicine ball or foam roller.

Coaching Points
Players should focus on using their shoulder muscles.

Purpose
To provide an overall running warm-up (and competition) for the entire team

Organization
Divide players into two groups. Group 1 is on offense; group 2 starts on defense. A coach is at home plate with a bat and a ball. The defense players need gloves and are divided up evenly between the left-field foul line and the right-field foul line, 30 yards (27.5 meters) from the fence.

Execution
Group 1 starts at home plate and will run the bases. The coach hits the ball anywhere on the softball field (right-field line, left-field line, backstop area, bunt area, and so on). Upon contact of the ball to the bat, one member of the offense team runs as many bases as possible before *both* the RF and LF members of group 2 touch the ball. Most players will get two or three bases. A defensive player may not push the ball closer to the other defensive player. Once all members of the offense have run once, switch groups.

Variation
Have players hit instead of using a coach.

Coaching Points
Make sure offensive players are making proper turns at the bases. Make sure defensive players use proper running form, even with their gloves on.

Chapter 2

Conditioning

Michelle Venturella   University of Iowa Associate Head Coach

Everyone knows that as you move up to the next level in any sport, the talent rises among players. Perhaps less obvious is that the range of skills among individual players narrows; that is, the players' physical abilities become more similar. This being the case, it's imperative that players find and exploit any advantage they can to give them their best chance at continued success. Improving their fitness level is one way to gain an advantage.

Playing softball requires explosiveness, acceleration, the ability to change directions, and a certain degree of endurance, so a comprehensive conditioning program for softball should include aerobic, strength, agility, and flexibility training. These components are best addressed via a conditioning program administered off the playing field, such as in a weight room with a strength and conditioning coach.

But there is more to the game of softball than athleticism and endurance. Softball requires players to perform softball-specific skills on the field both when they're fresh and when they're fatigued. Thus, the conditioning drills in this chapter have two purposes: to help delay the onset of fatigue in your players and to help them perform to the best of their ability even when fatigued.

Incorporating physical conditioning with technical, position-related training serves several purposes. First and foremost, the game gets quicker as the competition improves. Increasingly, what often separates good players from great ones is their level of conditioning as it relates to the game. Employing drills that improve play and conditioning simultaneously improves a player's ability to perform softball-specific skills with greater accuracy and quickness.

Second, well-conditioned players with softball-specific fitness have a much lower risk of injury than other players do. If you ask coaches to name their primary concern, season in and season out, many will say it's the health of their players. Injuries not only keep players out of games but prevent them from practicing with the sustained effort necessary to improve and raise their level of play. There's nothing less productive than a player hampered by nagging injuries such as pulls, strains, and sprains that never seem to fully heal over a season. Practicing gamelike situations at gamelike speeds conditions players' bodies to handle the physical stress of the athletic maneuvers required in softball. Although injuries can never be eliminated, a player's commitment to conditioning greatly reduces the negative impact of injuries over the course of her season or career.

Another purpose integrated physical and technical training serves is to increase mental toughness, an intangible trait closely associated to excellence and consistency. The mentally tough or clutch player can often overcome not only circumstance and fatigue but also a more talented opponent. What makes one player mentally tough and another mentally soft is not easy to determine, but certain methods can improve any player's mental toughness, regardless of talent level.

Most mental errors occur when players are fatigued or at critical stages during a game or season. The conditioning drills in this chapter will not only increase endurance but will put players in gamelike situations that simulate the mental stress that can occur during competition. Learning to deal with difficult conditions, such as fatigue and pressure, in practice makes playing through those circumstances in games more familiar and boosts the player's confidence that she can overcome them. Players who have succeeded at a certain task or in a certain situation are far more likely than others to be successful when faced with the same or a similar task or situation.

To create gamelike situations in practice, physical skills should be done in simulated game situations. For example, when players are working on base running, they should have a specific situation in mind so that they can picture where and how hard the ball was hit. This way, when a similar play happens in a game, they will know how to react. Another way to create gamelike situations is for coaches and teammates to simulate the strengths of future opponents. If batters face the types of pitches the next team's pitcher will throw, the batters will have an advantage in the game.

Much was said during the 2005 Women's College World Series championship game about Michigan's use of vision training. The training is based on the theory that a player who can hit a tennis ball moving at higher rates of speed and from different locations than what is normally seen in softball will be able to more quickly identify and hit a softball under game conditions. By putting players in a stressful, gamelike situation—even though the task was likely more difficult in and of itself—coaches created players who believed they could hit anything an opposing pitcher threw at them.

Finally, using drills in practice such as those you'll find in this chapter will create the competitive atmosphere that surrounds any championship team. A lack of competition tends to breed complacency, and a complacent team is often mediocre. Competition can be created within an individual drill and throughout practice. One player's hard work, determination, or success often infects other players competing in the same drill or game. It's no coincidence that every great rally or comeback started when a single player's effort ignited her teammates. Players tend to feed off each other, and raising the competitive bar in practice usually elevates the team's level of play come game time. Most players enjoy some competition in their drills. A spirited, competitive atmosphere during practice promotes team chemistry and can vastly improve an individual player's confidence level, which is probably the single most critical factor influencing the performance of any player.

As you can see, there are many reasons for including conditioning drills in practice. Some of these factors are more important to certain players because of what they individually bring to a team. For instance, one player might be mentally strong but in poor physical condition. Another might be confident but lacking a strong work ethic. These conditioning drills are great for touching on many areas critical to a team's success.

Purpose

To work on infield communication, footwork, and catching and receiving the ball

Organization

Start with players at their normal fielding positions. The catcher starts with the ball; there is no pitcher.

Execution

The ball starts at home. The SS starts the drill by breaking for 2B to receive the throw from the catcher, who is in a catcher's stance with ball in glove. When the ball is caught by the SS, the third baseman breaks for her base using proper footwork. The SS throws the ball to 3B. When the ball is caught by the third baseman, the first baseman breaks to receive the throw at 1B. She then throws the ball home to the catcher using proper footwork.

Variations

You can first execute this drill using either a force or tag situation. If you want to work on different infield throws, you can shorten the distance of the bases. Another variation is, after the first time through, to have each player stay at the base she's covering and throw a second ball into the drill. After the catcher throws the ball to 2B and the ball is then thrown to 3B, the SS should be ready to catch a second ball being thrown to her that has just been tossed into the drill by the coach. Make sure that players get back to their original starting positions each time because this enhances the conditioning aspect of the drill. Good communication is imperative in this drill.

Coaching Points

Watch players as they break for their base to make sure their footwork is correct. Also make sure they use proper technique when receiving the ball and that a quick transition is made.

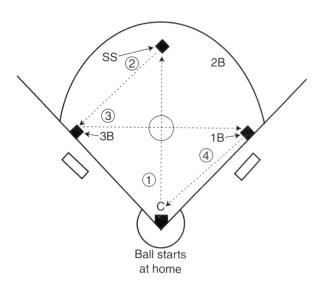

Ball starts
at home

19 CONTINUOUS BLOCKING

Purpose
To work on the catcher's reaction time and leg strength while using proper blocking technique

Organization
The catcher takes position in full equipment. Run this drill by home plate, if possible, though anywhere on the dirt will work fine. Use a stopwatch to assign a designated amount of time, or simply let your catcher know the number of sets and repetitions she needs to complete. The coach stands in front of the catcher with a ball in his or her hand; with the ball, the coach points in one of three directions: down, right, or left. No balls are thrown in this drill. You can start with two repetitions of 10 or go for 30 seconds and progress as you see fit. Limit this drill to two minutes. The key is to maintain proper technique despite fatigue.

Execution
The catcher starts in ready position (as if about to receive a pitch) and reacts to the direction indicated by the ball in the coach's hand. If the ball moves to the right, the catcher moves to her right and uses proper technique to block the imaginary ball. The catcher then gets up in that same spot and looks immediately for the next direction indicated by the ball in the coach's hand. The drill moves quickly because the catcher doesn't return to the original starting position each time.

Variations
Players can do this drill on their own. Just make sure they use proper technique. In this case, give them a number of reps to execute because keeping time themselves is difficult.

Coaching Points
Determine your catcher's weaker side for blocking and work that side more than the other.

Purpose

To work on the catcher's leg strength and quickness

Organization

The catcher should be in full gear. She can do this drill on her own with a set number of repetitions to execute (4 × 5 is a good goal to work up to, though this depends on the skill level of your catcher).

Execution

Starting in ready position (*a*), your catcher kicks her feet straight back so that her knees land in the place where her feet began (*b*). Then, from her block position she immediately tries to get her feet back underneath by swinging her arms forward, using momentum to get back up to ready position. Both knees should hit the ground at the same time. She shouldn't use her hands to help push off the ground to get back up. Emphasis is on how quickly she can execute the first part of this drill. When she kicks her feet back, her head should not come up, which would cause a slower movement when blocking the ball.

Variations

The toughest part of this drill is using momentum to get back to the feet, so emphasize only the first part of the drill, ensuring that your catcher uses proper technique in blocking. Let her get back to ready position as quickly as possible as she prepares to drop down again.

Coaching Points

Some catchers have trouble with this drill. Emphasize proper use of the arms as well as the concept that the quicker they can get back off their knees, the more momentum they'll have to help them get back to their start position. They might have to use their hands to push off of the ground until they gain enough strength to execute the drill properly.

Purpose

To work on outfielders' technique in fielding ground balls on the charge and proper footwork for catching fly balls hit over their heads

Organization

Set up two machines as close to home plate as possible but far enough out to allow for execution of the drill. Put a designated number of balls in a bucket, depending on how many reps you will complete. A ground ball and a fly ball is considered one rep. Start with two sets of four reps and work up.

Execution

Outfielders play at a depth from which they're able to throw a runner out at home. The ball machine throws a ground ball; an outfielder fields the ball and gets into throwing position, but then she tosses the ball off to the side. As she does so, a fly ball is coming at her from the ball machine. She must drop step and sprint to catch this ball or it will go over her head. She then returns to the start position and prepares for another rep.

Variations

To incorporate throwing into the drill, have outfielders throw home for the ground balls before sprinting back to catch the fly balls. Or, if you prefer, have them work on throws for the fly balls, using proper execution after catching the ball over their head. They can work on throws from both positions, but it is recommended that the throw following the fly ball go to 2B or 3B, depending on the situation you present to them. Remember that as fatigue sets in their throwing mechanics might be compromised.

Coaching Points

Watch for proper footwork as they come in to field the grounder and as they go back for the ball over their head. If a ball is off to one shoulder or the other, make sure they use proper technique and are efficient in getting rid of the ball.

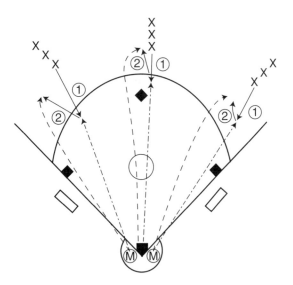

Purpose
To work on increasing players' range and to increase leg strength

Organization
Infield players start at their positions, as if a hitter is up to bat. Only one player at a time performs this drill. Have this player mark a line to indicate her starting position on the field. Have her mark another line about 10 feet (3 meters) in front of her.

Execution
A coach hits fungo from home plate. Infielders field the ball on the charge before the ball reaches the line they've marked in front of them. Players make the throw to 1B and then sprint back to their starting line. The coach then hits a Texas leaguer, forcing the same infielder to sprint to catch the ball. The grounder and the Texas leaguer are considered one rep. Do four reps, then move to another infielder. Each player executes the drill three times.

Variations
Yell out different situations so that players must vary the base they throw to after making the play. Use additional fields to complete the drill more quickly. If you do this, allow your players a couple of minutes to recover between sets of four.

Coaching Points
Give players sufficient time to get set in their starting positions so they use proper footwork when moving toward the ball. Use foul territory for some of the Texas leaguers to simulate game conditions.

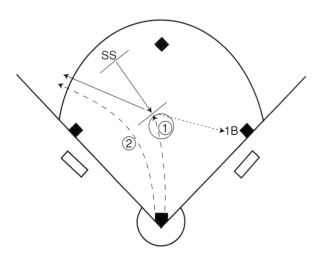

23   POP FOULS AND BUNTS

Purpose

To work on proper footwork for fielding a bunt and proper technique for fielding a pop foul

Organization

The catcher starts in full gear behind the plate in normal starting position. A coach needs a bucket of balls (or someone to feed him or her balls) to keep the drill moving. Two sets of four reps is a challenging starting point for this drill. Then work up in sets and repetitions as you see fit.

Execution

A coach stands behind the catcher with two balls. The catcher starts in ready position. Begin the drill by rolling the ball in front of the catcher to simulate a bunt. She fields the ball and throws to 1B using proper technique. After the throw she immediately gets back to ready position. The coach then stands in front of the catcher, just a few paces away, and tosses a ball into foul territory, simulating a pop foul. This toss should be thrown at various heights and distances. You can increase your catcher's range by making her go after pop-ups thrown far from her. The bunt and pop foul are considered one rep.

Variations

It's important to work the bunting game to all bases. You might want to vary the situation for each rep (e.g., no one on base, runner at 1B, runners at 1B and 2B, etc.). Another variation is how you toss the pop-up. You can stand in front of the player with two balls in your hand right in front of the catcher's mask. Move one of the balls away, and the catcher will immediately move in that direction for a foul pop-up. You then immediately toss the ball in the air into foul territory on that side, and the catcher can pick up the ball.

Coaching Points

Encourage catchers to catch foul balls with their mask on because time is lost in removing the mask and new catcher's masks have fewer blind spots. The time it takes for a catcher to remove the mask and pick up the ball can be costly if it is a low-trajectory foul ball. Also, be sure to teach your catchers to "give" with the catch as they catch pop fouls from underneath the ball. Many times catchers try to reach for the ball, which causes it to pop out of their glove because of the amount of spin on the ball.

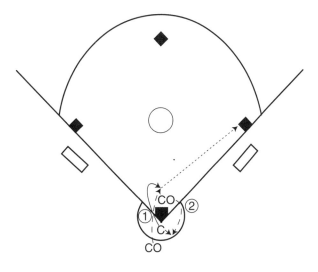

Purpose

To have infielders work on the kinds of throws that occur in a game

Organization

To maximize the conditioning aspect of this drill, use multiple groups of four and don't have players follow their throws (alternatively, you can stack two players at each corner and have them follow their throws). You need only one ball for this drill, but you might want to have extras off to the side in case of errant throws. Infielders start in box formation about 20 feet (6 meters) apart from one another.

Execution

Start with the ball in the glove of player A, who begins the drill. Player A runs a few steps and then tosses the ball *from her glove* to player B. Player A then runs back to her starting position, ready to receive the ball as it makes its way around. This is a glove-to-glove toss. The ball continues around to each player two times and then switches directions, still using the same toss. After each player has run both directions twice, the players should back out away from each other so that they now make a box and are about 30 feet (9 meters) from each other. The next round uses a forehand and backhand underhand flip (the kind of toss a third baseman uses to throw to the catcher on a squeeze play). Again, this will be done going both directions, which means the backhand flip will be used as well. After running both directions twice, all players move back 10 feet (3 meters) again, and work on the 3/4 throw begins. After working both directions for the 3/4 throw, players again back up 10 feet and begin

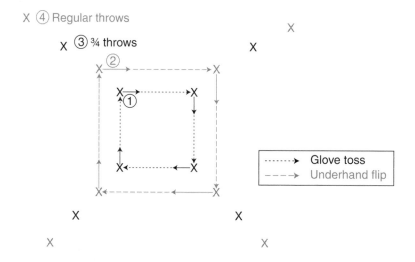

throwing normal overhand throws. Each player should throw to an inside and outside target to work on their different footwork. Each time a player is going to receive a ball, she needs to communicate to the player throwing to her and show her a target.

Variations

The variations will depend on the level you're coaching. It might not be necessary for younger players to work on the first part of the drill (the glove toss). You might simply start with the underhand toss and work on their footwork, and proceed from there.

Coaching Points

The reason to use both directions in this drill is to help work on the proper footwork needed to execute these throws properly. One way or the other is typically easier for each player. As you're watching the drill, notice your players' strengths and weaknesses; this is information that will help you plan your practices.

Purpose

To work on proper footwork and the angles necessary for an outfielder to chase down a ball over her head; to work on running hard after the ball

Organization

The coach has a bucket of balls and stands about 15 to 20 feet (4.5 to 6 meters) in front of an outfielder, who's in her normal starting position (left field, right field, or centerfield). If you want to put all your outfielders in one position to save time, you can do that, but it's best if each player at some point gets the chance to do this drill from her regular position.

Execution

The coach starts the drill by signaling which direction the player should turn and calling out "go!" Using proper footwork (the drop step), the player breaks for the ball. The coach throws the ball into the air to simulate a pop-up. The ball should be tossed in such a fashion that the outfielder can sprint to the spot where the ball is going to land and arrive just before the ball does. This simulates catching a ball on the run, although here the player does not catch the ball. The other way to execute the drill is to have the player do the same thing except actually sprint to the spot, get around the ball, and then let it fall just in front of her. This teaches the player to position her body behind the ball on a fly so she has the momentum she needs to make a throw. In this case, the coach needs to toss the ball higher to give the player ample time.

Variations

You can also work this as a "beat the ball to the fence" drill by simply moving your outfielders into a deeper position in the outfield. Consider running the drill as a competition drill to see how many balls they can get to. The difficulty of the drill depends entirely on how the ball is tossed.

Coaching Points

Most players have a stronger side. As you're running the drill, work each player's weaker side to help her gain confidence on that side. Watch for proper running technique. Some players tend to put their gloves out when they run. If the glove comes up too soon, speed is lost.

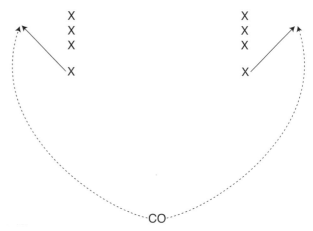

Purpose

For infielders to work on basic fielding technique and to develop mental toughness

Organization

Each fielder starts at her position. The catcher stands in and feeds the balls to the coach, who is hitting fungo. You can use your outfielders to fill in off to the side in foul territory to ensure that balls are quickly getting back to the coach so the drill doesn't break down. All throws go to 1B.

Execution

The coach starts by hitting balls at the third baseman. Most balls are either right at the fielder or a step or two in either direction or up in front. The idea is to keep hitting at the player until you can tell her legs are getting fatigued, which will vary for each player. Players might field between 15 and 25 balls depending on their level of conditioning. After you get a sense of what is a good goal for your team, make the drill competitive by giving players a number to reach that will be extremely challenging. After the third baseman has had her turn, next is the SS, second baseman, first baseman, and catcher. With the catcher you can use bunts to throw to 1B.

Variations

Mix in the short game. This is harder than just the grounders because they'll have to move more. It's good to keep this drill like a game, however. Corner players usually go only a step or two in either direction, so you might choose to hit their rounds accordingly, whereas middle infielders must cover more ground.

Coaching Points

This is a great drill for the end of practice. The energy from the team should be apparent. Have the team cheer each player on as she executes the drill. Balls should be hit in a quick manner but with enough time to let players get back to their start position.

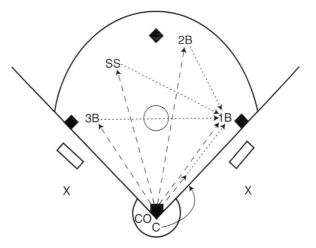

Purpose

To work on fielding balls in the 5/6 hole; to train proper communication and technique when receiving a ball at 2B

Organization

The coach needs a bucket of balls to hit fungo from home. Fielders involved are the SS, first baseman, and second baseman.

Execution

Have the SS start in her normal fielding position. The coach hits the ball in the 5/6 hole. The SS fields the ball properly, throws to 1B, and then sprints to 2B to receive a ball hit to the second baseman by the coach. As the player approaches 2B, make sure she's calling for the ball and showing a target so that the second baseman knows where she's throwing the ball. Give the SS a chance to get back in position and then repeat the drill for a set of five reps (one rep equals fielding a ball and receiving a ball).

Variations

Add one more step by making the play be a double play and having the SS come across the bag to throw to 1B.

Coaching Points

Monitor how much throwing you want your players to do, especially if they're making long throws to 1B from the 5/6 hole. Remember they'll get fatigued doing this drill and tend to lose their technique. If you find that a set of five is too much or not enough, adjust accordingly.

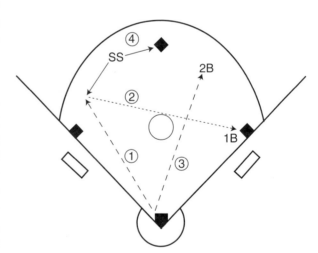

Purpose

To work on proper technique in using the forehand and backhand flip

Organization

You need a SS and first baseman to receive balls from the second baseman. Have a bucket of balls at home plate, where the coach will hit fungo. You also need a player to feed balls to the coach.

Execution

The coach hits the ball to the 3/4 hole so that the player must field the ball and flip it to 1B for the out. The second baseman quickly gets back in her starting position to field a ball that the coach hits up the middle. Depending on the position of the fielder, she'll use either a forehand or backhand flip to the SS, who is covering 2B.

Variations

For a higher level player, work the glove toss on either the ball to the 3/4 hole or up the middle.

Coaching Points

When performing these drills it's important to have players thinking about the situations that these mimic in a game. For example, in the first part of this drill no one is on base. The second part of the drill would have a runner at 1B. The more you can incorporate actual situations into practice, the more comfortable your players will be when preplanning in a game.

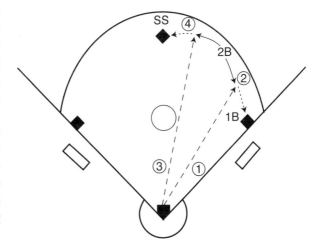

Purpose

To have pitchers work on loading position, leg drive, and focus, while catchers work on transitioning the ball out of the glove and throwing back to the pitcher's throwing shoulder

Organization

The pitcher and catcher start about 40 to 45 feet (12 to 13.5 meters) apart from one another. The starting distance needs to be a few steps beyond the actual pitching distance because the pitcher will walk into her pitch and release the ball rather than start in a normal starting position on the mound. The catcher should be in full gear minus her mask but will be in a standing position for this drill. Players usually start with two sets of 10 reps. Each week increase the number of sets and repetitions, as long as the drill is running properly, eventually topping out at three sets of 15 reps or three sets at 30 seconds each.

Execution

When the pitcher is ready she'll start the drill by walking into her pitch and pitching the ball to the catcher, who is ready to receive the ball in an athletic position with her glove open to give a good target at about chest height. The catcher should be constantly talking and encouraging the pitcher throughout the drill, including counting the number of repetitions for her out loud. As soon as the pitcher releases the ball, she immediately gets back to her original starting position, facing the catcher the entire time, and gets ready to receive the ball being thrown back from the catcher. One of the objectives for the catcher is to work on quick footwork as well as a quick release to throw the ball back to the pitcher on her glove side so the pitcher doesn't lose any momentum in the drill.

Variations

The speed of the drill is the main factor that will vary. You can do this at half or three-quarter speed until both the pitcher and catcher have a good feel for the drill.

Coaching Points

Make sure the pitcher's arm circle remains consistent. Sometimes the momentum causes the arm to stray off line.

Purpose

To work on proper base-running techniques designated at each base while capitalizing on errors made by the defense or by simply challenging the defense by allowing runners to advance to the next base

Organization

Split up your team so you have an even number of players at home, 1B, and 3B. A coach stands on the mound to simulate the pitcher. Have one player stand in foul territory by 1B with a bucket of balls to simulate a throw getting away from the first baseman, and have another player stand on the foul side of 3B to simulate a throw kicking off the third baseman on an attempted pick-off from the catcher.

Execution

The coach simulates a pitch. The runner at home runs to 1B as if she has hit a base hit in the infield. She runs through the base and looks toward foul territory. The player with the bucket of balls rolls a ball toward the fence, and the runner takes off for 2B and hits her slide. At the same time, the runner at 1B has a hit and run on. This runner is trying to challenge the RF and the preciseness of her throw. She visualizes the ball hit behind her and picks up the coach at 3B, who's waving her around and signaling her to slide or to stop on the base. The final component uses the runner at 3B. She takes a lead and acts as if the catcher throws down to pick her off. The runner dives back into the base with her head facing foul territory. She picks up the player standing in foul territory to see if this player tosses a ball off to the side to simulate a ball kicking off the glove of the third baseman. If so, the runner quickly gets up and scores. Run a circuit at least two or three times for each player at each base to have a good training effect.

Variations

You don't need to have players standing off to the side. You can simply explain what each starting position represents, and players can visualize the ball being overthrown or being hit behind them or being tipped off the fielder's glove.

Coaching Points

Trying to get players to think about situations in a game is critical. Make sure to reiterate to your players that they need to literally see the ball so that their reactions are more realistic and gamelike.

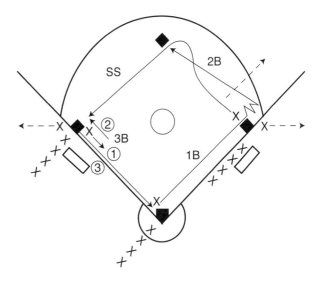

Fundamental Skills Drills

Chapter 3

Catching

Deanna Gumpf Notre Dame Head Coach

In softball, the skill of catching is equal in importance to batting, throwing, and running. Almost every out in the game of softball is made through means of a catch of some sort, be it a catcher catching a third strike, a force play at a base, a routine out at first base, a tag play at second base, third base, or home, or catching a line drive or fly ball hit into the air by a batter. Catching and throwing are the two most important aspects of defense in softball, and if the correct techniques and fundamentals are not well learned, disaster will strike. Always remember what most coaches agree on: Offense wins games, but defense wins championships.

Catching can be intimidating for some players initially. Eliminating or at least reducing timidity and fear is the first priority for a coach when working with inexperienced players. To reduce players' fear and to make many of the catching drills easier, use balls other than regulation softballs. For beginners, use soft (RIF), light balls (Wiffle or tennis balls work well), or large rubber balls that are softer and easier to catch. As fear diminishes, progress to using regulation softballs. In the early stages, players should learn to catch and field without a glove as they pick up the basics of catching. Once they have a solid catching foundation, progress players to catching and fielding with a glove.

The art of catching is a series of incremental steps that enables players to build on previous successes. These incremental steps use a combination of many variables. The techniques are best taught through adjusting these variables within the catching drills. The areas for which variables are essential are:

1. Receiving hand (bare hand, board or paddle, and the standard glove)
2. Velocity of the throw (soft, medium, or hard)
3. Various directions or angles of the throw (above the head, face, chest, belt, knees, feet, and to each side of the defensive player)
4. Difficulty factor (extend drills to test your players' limits, but always attempt to keep them "just within reach" rather than "just out of reach")

5. Number of repetitions to build successful execution of technique (the drills in this chapter don't suggest a set number of repetitions because number or reps should be based on each coach's requirements and the incremental improvements of the players)

Several common and basic drills are not included in this chapter's drill section but can be taught during practice situations. These drills and situations include the following:

Side to side: A partner drill in which players roll a ball back and forth, shuffling their feet to keep the ball in front of the body when taking the ball in.

Short hops: A partner drill in which partners at close range (10 to 20 feet, 3 to 6 meters) throw one-hop balls to each other to work on soft hands and collecting the ball out in front at the center of the body.

Sun balls: A coach hits or throws balls at players into the sun so they learn how to use their glove to shield the sun or to play the ball out of the sun for a successful catch.

Diving head-first catch: For infielders and outfielders; use diving mats until players are experienced in this drill.

Double-play simulations: Players catch, transfer from glove to hand, then move toward the throwing location.

Catch-and-tag simulation on a pick-off or steal attempt: Players catch a thrown ball and quickly move their glove to a target, such as a base or cone.

Running with the glove: All defensive players should learn to sprint without extending their glove hand until the ball arrives. One good method is to have players wear their fielding gloves at practice when running bases or during running drills.

It will be extremely helpful to you as a coach if every defensive play in the game of softball is simulated in some way through drills. There are many kinds of drills to work on for each defensive position, but almost every defensive drill demonstrates the correct method of catching the ball. This chapter is full of drills to improve the skill of catching, starting with the very basic drills and moving to more involved and advanced catching drills. A general principle when it comes to any defensive catching drill is that "the ball always comes first."

31 TENNIS BALL BOUNCE

Purpose
To improve players' ability to concentrate on catching a bounced ball and to quickly transfer the ball to the throwing hand; to improve eye–hand coordination and using soft hands

Organization
Pair up players one on one (or one coach with one player). For the basic difficulty level, use one tennis ball for each pair of partners. For the intermediate and advanced levels, use two balls per pair.

Execution
Two players stand across from each other about 10 to 15 feet (3 to 4.5 meters) apart. With her throwing hand, one player bounces or skips the tennis ball to the other player. The ball is thrown so that it bounces near the midpoint between the two players. This way, the ball can be caught on its downward arc. The ball should be thrown at an angle so that it bounces near the body. The player receiving the ball catches it with the glove hand only, then immediately transfers the ball to her throwing hand and repeats the drill in the opposite direction.

Variations
The height and direction of the bounce can make this drill more difficult. Intermediate players should both throw tennis balls at the same time to get twice the repetitions. Have intermediate players bounce the ball at a point two thirds the distance between the two. The ball should be thrown to each side of the player but should remain fairly near the body. Advanced players should simultaneously throw balls to each other and receive throws at an extended side-to-side location. Have these players throw the balls harder and lower.

Coaching Points
This drill is typically run with infielders but is helpful to all defensive players. For maximum benefit, attempt to pair up players of equal ability. The more often players do this drill, the better their catch, transfer, and throw rhythm and technique become.

Purpose

To improve on using "soft hands" when receiving a ground ball; to help players focus on keeping hands out in front of the body when receiving a ground ball; to assist players in learning to absorb the ball via a two-hand collection; to help eliminate any tendency to "stab" at the ball when attempting to catch; to help players learn proper technique when using the backhand side of the glove or when the forehand side is fully extended

Organization

For this drill, you'll need a bucket of balls (tennis balls, softies, or real balls) and a paddle. Organize players in pairs, with a coach advising, or partner a coach with each player.

Execution

The player starts in a defensive ready position about 20 feet (6 meters) from the coach. If the pair consists of a coach and a player, the coach starts by rolling softie balls to the player. The player collects the ground ball by using the paddle as a glove. The player should focus on receiving the ball with two hands and on keeping hands out in front of the body using good form and mechanics. If players are performing the drill correctly, their hands should never sting when receiving the ball. If two players are doing the drill, a coach assists as needed.

Variations

As players become more comfortable or advanced, balls can be rolled or hit harder and bounced toward the players. The coach might also incorporate angles when hitting the balls, which allows players to work on footwork to the ball and to focus on proper mechanics when fielding with a paddle. This drill can also be done from a backhand position or from an extended forehand position. When working at these two extremes, players should try only to stop the ball (because only one hand can be used). When stopped properly, the ball should return toward the direction from which it was thrown.

Coaching Points

There are several types of commercial paddles, including "The Practice Glove" or "Soft Hands," that can be purchased through softball or baseball vendors. You can also make an 8-by-8-inch (20-by-20-centimeter) paddle with a tape grip across the center point that holds the hand on the paddle. Less experienced players can use Ping-Pong paddles and tennis balls for this drill. If using Ping-Pong paddles, players should hold the paddle near the top of the handle so that the thumb is less likely to be hit with the ball.

Make sure that your players' fingers are pointing down when receiving ground balls. For beginners, start with a tennis ball or softie ball and work up to using a real ball. Use the variations as players become more advanced.

Purpose

To work on different angles when catching pop-ups and fly balls over either shoulder at all angles

Organization

You'll need one coach, two to six players, and five cones for each starting point; starting points are set at about 9, 11, 12, 1, and 3 o'clock, with the coach at clock center. Use one ball for each player in the drill plus a few extra near the coach at a reachable distance. Run this drill in a grass area about the size of the dirt portion of an infield. To begin the drill, the coach stands in a stationary position; players stand in a line and begin at the immediate left side (9 o'clock) of the coach about 25 feet (7.6 meters) away.

Execution

Each player starts with a ball. The first player throws her ball to the coach and begins to run back away from the coach to her left at an angle. The coach then throws the ball over the player's left shoulder to simulate a fly ball or blooper over her head to the left side. The player catches the ball and then proceeds to the next starting point. The entire line of players follows and completes this catching progression. The first player then starts at about 11 o'clock position and repeats the process. Repeat again from 12 o'clock. Now players will be directly in front of the coach, about 25 feet away. This line then continues at about 1 o'clock and 3 o'clock. After players have completed the five lines of catching over the left shoulder, they start at the immediate right of the coach and move from 3 o'clock back to 9 o' clock, catching balls over the right shoulder.

Variations

In smaller spaces this drill can be used to practice catching bloopers or line drives while players are running to the ball behind them at an angle. For beginners, use softie balls (RIF 1 or RIF 5) or tennis balls to help reduce fear. For more advanced players, use real balls and change the speed and arc of the throw to exaggerate deeper angles for outfielders and shorter angles for infielders (bloopers, high fly balls, deeper balls, and so on).

Coaching Points

This is a great warm-up drill for outfielders before working on fly balls and ground balls. You can also use it as an agility drill. The main areas to focus on are (1) footwork when taking an angle on a ball thrown behind them and (2) running while pumping both arms until reaching for the ball to catch it. Some players run toward fly balls with their catching arm extended. This drill helps players gain confidence in their abilities to catch a ball while running and sprinting to a fly ball that's over their head. There's no standard starting distance for the drill. How close players start from each other depends on the space available or their defensive position.

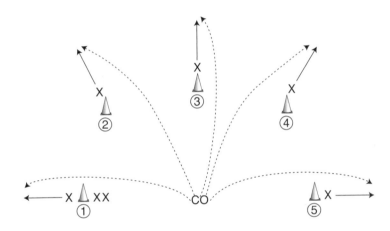

Purpose

To teach a player to catch a thrown ball or line drive effectively while running at full speed

Organization

This drill requires two to six players (each with a ball) and an area from as small as 30 feet (9 meters) to as big as half of the outfield, depending on the variation. The coach stands about 30 feet in front of the players to start the drill. Each player starts with a ball. The coach starts the drill with a ball in hand, ready to throw.

Execution

A player throws her ball to the coach and then sprints across at the angle designated by the coach. The player doesn't begin to sprint until the coach receives the thrown ball. As the player is sprinting, the coach throws the ball toward the player so that she's reaching to catch the ball on the run. After the line of players is complete, they begin in the general area in which the last ball was caught and start over, going back in the opposite direction. By running in both directions, players work on receiving balls on both sides of the body.

Each catch should be a different type, simulating all sorts of hit balls. How the balls are thrown will determine what type of catch you want players to work on. Throw the balls so that your players are sprinting back for a fly ball over their heads, sprinting in for a short fly ball, and sprinting straight across for a line drive.

Variations

Players start about 90 feet (27.5 meters) from the coach. One player throws the ball at the coach and immediately begins to sprint straight toward the coach. As the coach receives the ball thrown from the player, the coach then throws his or her own ball back at the player. The player receives the ball and continues sprinting toward the coach. The player immediately throws the ball back to the coach, still sprinting toward the coach. Repeat once more or until the player is right in front of the coach. The goal is to attempt to achieve at least three exchanges. The final step in this drill is to have the player run around the coach and continue sprinting back to where she started. The coach will throw the ball over the player's head, simulating an over-the-head pop-up.

Coaching Points

You can also use this drill for conditioning. The coach should throw the ball just within reach, if possible. It's important that the coach has a plan for each type of throw he or she throws to the player. Coaches can simulate a line drive or a thrown ball by having players run straight across in both directions. Players will need to extend their gloves to the limit. The coach might throw the ball so that the player must reach behind her, thus simulating a bad throw. You can simulate deep fly balls by having players start close and run out at a deep angle; you can simulate weak pop-ups by starting players deep and having them run in at an angle.

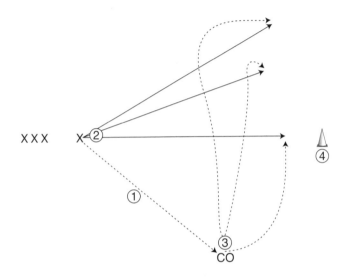

Purpose

To improve reaction time and eye–hand coordination for all defensive players

Organization

You'll need a bucket of balls. A coach and a player, or two players, pair off. One player should stand just in front of some type of barrier, such as a screen, fence, or backstop (because some of the thrown balls will go past her). The coach or second player stands about 15 to 20 feet (4.5 to 6 meters) from the first player.

Execution

The coach or partner throws overhand throws at the player in several directions, including over her head left and right, below her waist left and right, and belt high left and right. There's no sequence or exact location for the throws. The player attempts to catch every ball wherever it's thrown, and then she drops the ball to either side. All balls are collected when the thrower's bucket is empty.

Variations

The experience level of the player determines the distance between the coach and player and the type of ball to use. Beginners stand 20 to 25 feet (6 to 7.5 meters) apart, using Wiffle or softie balls. Intermediate players stand 15 to 20 feet apart and use real balls. Advanced players use real balls, throwing hard throws from 10 to 15 feet (3 to 4.5 meters) apart.

Coaching Points

This is a great reaction drill for all skill levels. Because players receiving the ball tend to watch the thrower's eyes to determine the direction of the throw, the thrower sometimes needs to look in another direction from that in which the ball will be thrown. For advanced players, throw many balls just outside of their throwing-side toe because this is a very difficult location. This drill is most beneficial for infielders but also works great for pitchers' reactions to balls hit straight back at them on the mound.

Purpose

To promote communication skills and calling the ball; to build competitiveness; to improve diving intuition; to help create or initiate a quick first step

Organization

You'll need a coach, two fielders, four cones, and a bucket of balls. Mark off an area 10 feet (3 meters) by 10 feet with the cones to make boundaries for the drill. Standing at the front of the square, the coach has a bucket of balls directly to the side in easy reach. The two fielders stand inside the square, either side by side or front to back.

Execution

The drill begins with the coach throwing the ball in the air inside the square. One of the fielders calls the ball, catches it, and tosses it outside the square; she then gets ready for the next toss from the coach. While that fielder is calling for the ball, the other fielder is looking for the next ball being tossed up to be caught. In the event that a fielder dives for a ball, the coach does *not* wait for her to get up from the ground or to get back in ready position before throwing the next ball. The goal of the drill is to get the fielders to communicate and avoid going after the same ball. The coach should make fielders move to all locations within the square, diving to the side, catching balls over their heads, and diving for balls in front of them.

Variations

This drill can be as easy or as difficult as you want to make it. The level of difficulty depends on the throws from the coach. The square can be made larger to force fielders to cover more area.

Coaching Points

Make sure fielders are tossing balls outside the square to avoid injuries caused by stepping or diving on a ball. The coach should toss balls only within the boundaries of the square.

Purpose

To work on maintaining a good balance while running, keeping the eyes on the ball, and receiving the ball while in constant motion

Organization

Players organize into groups of four. Each group uses four cones to create a square about 30 feet (9 meters) by 30 feet. Each player starts just outside of a cone.

Execution

One player begins with a ball. On the coach's command, players begin running in a clockwise rotation around the cones. Players begin to throw the ball around the square, one player at a time in the same direction in which they're running. They continue to catch and throw in the square until the coach whistles. At that time, the players stop, change directions, and continue the drill counterclockwise.

Variations

Set the square up with a player at each cone. Without running, players throw and catch around the square in both directions. Players should focus on switching their feet to receive the ball and then to throw the ball. Make sure players' feet are constantly moving and remaining balanced in the direction of the catch and the throw.

Another variation is to move the cones closer or further away, depending on which receiving and throwing techniques you want to work on. If you move the cones closer, players can simulate catching the ball and tagging the cone as if it's a base or home plate. They can also work on backhand tosses and short underhand throws. If you move the cones farther apart, the player catching the ball gets more difficult opportunities because throws are more erratic.

Coaching Points

Players have a tendency to collapse the square as they execute the drill. Remind them that a consistent square needs to be maintained. This drill is also good for conditioning because players begin to run faster around the circle. Make sure players stay focused on the ball while staying as close to the cones as possible.

Purpose

To practice the low catch and improve the decision-making process for balls hit in front of the defensive player (bloop hits or short pop-ups)

Organization

The drill requires 5 to 10 balls, three cones, two to six players, a coach, and an area about 60 feet (18 meters) in length. Set a cone at each end of the 60-foot area to designate the starting points. Place the third cone at the midpoint; the coach will run the drill from here.

Execution

Players begin at the designated starting point; the coach kneels at the halfway point of the two cones. The first player sprints toward the coach. As the player approaches, the coach tosses the ball straight up into the air about two to three feet (about one meter) off the ground. In a full sprint, the player tries to catch the ball in the air before it drops to the ground. After the catch is made, the player slows down, tosses the ball back to the coach, and jogs straight ahead to the cone in front of her. This cone becomes the starting point for the next phase of the drill. Players continue to go back and forth until the coach calls an end to the drill.

Variation

Let the ball bounce before players are allowed to catch it so they can practice running through the ball.

Coaching Points

For beginners, adjust the toss so that players are more comfortable in sprinting to the ball and making the catch in the air. This will also teach them to run through the catch. For more advanced players, make the toss very challenging, forcing them to decide whether to dive or to try to catch the ball on the run. The less air time the toss has, the more difficult the catch and decision-making process will be. Take care in determining the experience level of your players and in judging which players should attempt a head-first dive. This is an effective drill without using the dive.

Purpose

To allow defensive players to practice catching balls near or at a barrier (e.g., backstop, foul-line fence, outfield fence) without incurring an injury; to reduce players' fear of catching close to a barrier

Organization

The drill requires a fence, screen, wall, net, or backstop. (Indoors, use a wall or a net.) You'll also need 10 to 20 balls (depending on the number of players). The coach stands near the barrier. Players line up either to the side or in front of the chosen barrier. The starting distance varies depending on which position players are participating in the drill. Outfielders start about 20 feet (6 meters) from the barrier, lined up to the side or in front of the barrier. Infielders also start about 20 feet away from the barrier, lined up to the side or behind the barrier. Catchers start about 15 feet (4.5 meters) from the barrier in a squat position with the barrier behind them.

Execution

The coach throws the ball toward the barrier. The player facing the coach reacts to the thrown ball and sprints toward the barrier. She then tries to find the barrier while keeping her eye on the ball to make the catch. Her goal is to successfully catch the ball while using good technique to handle the barrier. There are two best techniques to use. If there's enough time to reach the barrier, the player should hit or touch the barrier first with the glove hand to stop the body's momentum; she should then switch hands to feel the barrier with the throwing hand and use the glove hand to catch the ball. When time

is too short to reach the barrier and catch the ball without crashing into the barrier, the player should slide feet first before catching the ball.

Variations

The distance of the players from the barrier and the arc of the throws are the key factors when modifying this drill.

Coaching Points

It usually takes a few attempts by the coach to get the correct distance, angle, and elevation on the thrown ball. Because of the difficulty of the throw by the coach, a low percentage of catching attempts are successful. The coach might wish to toss the ball in an underhand motion for greater accuracy.

Purpose

To incorporate different receiving techniques and to challenge players' speed and aggressiveness in receiving balls

Organization

This drill requires two cones, four balls, and a large area (about half of the outfield). One coach and all players participate one at a time. The fielder begins in the middle of the triangle, with the coach at the bottom tip of the triangle. Cones are placed at the top left and right points of the triangle.

Execution

The fielder sprints toward the coach, who is at the tip or bottom of the triangle, and the coach tosses a ball for a diving or shoestring catch. The fielder makes the catch and tosses the ball back to the coach. The fielder then takes off running toward the left top point of the triangle, and the coach throws a fly ball over the player's left shoulder to force an over-the-shoulder catch. The fielder makes the catch and then immediately runs around the cone and makes a good throw back to the coach. The coach then rolls a ground ball toward the player near the left cone. This player sprints toward the ball, fields it, and makes a good throw back to the coach. She then sprints toward the coach for another shoestring catch. The fielder repeats this process on the right side of the triangle, again ending the drill sprinting toward the coach and making a final diving catch.

Variations

Adjust the distance of the triangle to simulate specific positions. To make the drill more difficult, have players run continuously in both legs of the triangle.

Coaching Points

This drill can be suitable for any skill level, depending on the throws and on how quickly your players are completing it. Players should focus on running while pumping both arms until it's time to reach for the catch.

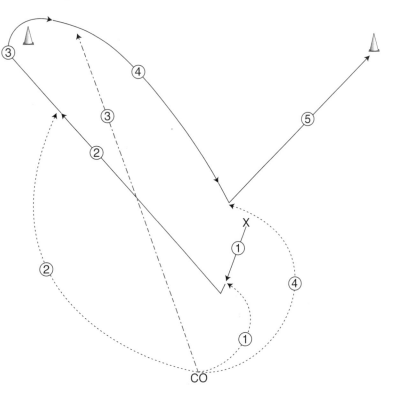

Purpose

To help infielders feel comfortable and confident in receiving all types of throws while defending their position; to help players understand that no matter where the throw is, the ball comes first!

Organization

Use a standard field setup with an infielder at her position. A coach with a bucket of balls (and a bat, if necessary) either hits or throws balls from various areas of the field to the infielders.

Execution

The coach stands at various places on the field, depending on the starting position of the player. For example, if the coach begins the drill with the first baseman, the coach can stand in the general area of the SS or 3B. On command, the player at 1B goes to the 1B bag to receive the thrown or hit ball from the coach. The player's goal is to catch the ball no matter where it's thrown. At the same time, she is trying to focus on good footwork to the base. Once the player has received the ball, she tosses it to the side, out of her way; she then receives the next throw from the coach.

For plays at 2B and 3B, the coach can stand in various areas in the outfield and hit to the second baseman, shortstop, or third baseman defending each base. This simulates bad throws coming from the outfield. Again, each player focuses on making a clean play out of the throw while working on defensive footwork and a tag at the base. For the catcher, this drill provides great practice for blocking at home plate. The coach can hit or throw balls to the catcher from all areas of the infield and outfield.

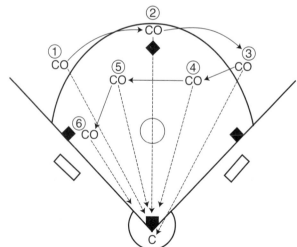

Coaching Points

This drill is useful for all skill levels and helps to reduce fear of the ball in critical situations. Bat control for the coach is critical. The coach should have control over the strength and the direction of the hit or thrown ball. This drill helps players to build confidence in their ability to defend a poorly thrown ball from other players on the field. Players should focus on footwork and glove work at each base and home plate.

Chapter 4

Throwing

Louie Berndt *Florida State University Associate Head Coach*

It's the seventh inning, the score is tied with two outs, and the winning run is on second. A routine grounder is hit to the shortstop . . . and she overthrows the first baseman. The runner on second scores, and the game is over. Like many games, this game was lost because of one simple throwing error.

Practicing and perfecting the throw is obviously essential to the game of softball. Coaches must focus on throwing consistency during warm-up and through drill work. The fundamentals of the game should be taught and reinforced daily in practice. A student of the game can't improve on her ability if she doesn't practice the skills of her sport. If your pitcher makes one ill-advised throw to the plate, if your catcher makes one wide throw to second base, or if your normally reliable shortstop sails her throw over your first baseman's head, the game can be over. When it comes to softball, there's not much worse for a coach than seeing a game end this way. Making consistently accurate throws is as big a part of the game as any.

It is always interesting to watch high school and summer ball teams conduct their warm-ups and practices. It seems every player wants to hit or field the ball, but no one wants to work on perfecting throws. Although throwing is a basic skill of the game, it's often ignored or skipped over during practice. Some teams spend little time throwing when warming up prior to a game or practice. Of course other teams, the more organized and structured teams, go through an elaborate throwing procedure before taking the field. These are the teams that win championships.

Every player must learn to execute the task of throwing from all playing positions, and this is especially important when working with younger players. Coaches must focus teaching drills and the explanations of the drills to the level of the player they're working with. For example, some coaches tend to forget about the size of a young player's hand. Very young players will need to practice with smaller balls, such as tennis balls or soft baseballs. With proper techniques and consistent training, throwing is a skill that can easily be performed by players of all ages.

Challenging your players as they progress will help them stay involved in practice and keep their heads in the game. As you continue in this chapter, remember to be creative when teaching each drill. Each player is unique and needs to be treated so. You can modify the drills to challenge your more advanced players and to allow your lower-skilled players a better chance for success. Learning a skill can be quite a challenge for novice players, but they seem to pick things up more quickly when the rest of the team is performing the same or a similar task. Always emphasize proper mechanics when performing these drills. Make some of them competitive. Competition always seems to work like magic.

This chapter includes many throwing drills, from novice to advanced. It also covers different types of throws, from the outfield to infield to underhand tosses. Use these drills daily in practice. Each one provides a different gamelike setting to give your players the experience they need to avoid being caught off guard in game situations.

42   WRIST SNAPS

Purpose
To work on proper grip when throwing a softball

Organization
Each player stands across from a partner, no more than eight feet (2.4 meters) apart (shorten the distance for beginning players). When all players are standing across from their partners, two parallel lines should be formed: line A and line B. For safety, make sure that players in each line are two to three feet (about a meter) apart. The partners in one line start with the ball in their throwing hand using a proper grip.

Execution
Using a proper grip, players in line A snap their ball to their partners in line B. When players have the proper grip, they can snap the ball to their partner focusing on the rotation of the seams. Partners continue to snap the ball back and forth for a total of 10 throws.

Variations
Use tennis balls for younger players or players with smaller hands. Increase the distance between players to challenge them more and to multiply the revolutions of the ball. Players can work on this drill alone, without partners, by lying down on their backs with their throwing arms in front of them at a 90-degree angle (see next drill).

Coaching Points
Make sure that the pads of your players' fingers are on the seams. Emphasize the ball rolling off the fingertips; players should not grip the ball in their palm. The wrist should be cocked back and snap with a 12 o'clock to 6 o'clock rotation—a movement similar to shooting a free throw in basketball. Make sure your players are using only their wrists to make their throws. If balls seem to be tailing off, players are probably turning their wrists to the left or right. You want the ball to have a slight flight pattern during the throw (i.e., throws should not be line drives).

Purpose

To practice using a proper grip when throwing a softball

Organization

Players work alone, lying on their backs. Make sure they are in a line and about five to six feet (1.5 to 2 meters) apart for safety purposes. Equipment for this drill may include a ball or a spinner.

Execution

Using the proper grip, each player snaps the ball directly up in the air, focusing on the rotation of the seams. Each player snaps the ball 10 times.

Variations

Have players work on varying the height of the toss (e.g., high, medium, or low). Use tennis balls for younger players or those with smaller hands.

Coaching Points

Make sure the pads of the fingers are on the seams. Focus on the ball rolling off the finger tips and on snapping the wrist rather than using the elbow to push the ball up and forward. Make sure players are using only their wrists. If the ball is going toward their feet, they're probably pushing the ball forward. If the ball is going behind their head, they're probably extending their elbow backward rather than snapping their wrist. You want the ball to have a slight flight pattern rather than be a straight line drive.

44 WRIST SNAPS USING A STRIPED BALL

Purpose
To continue working on the proper wrist snap and ball rotation

Organization
Players work in partners standing about eight feet (2.4 meters) apart from one another. Vary the distance between partners depending on their skill level. Players should form two parallel lines of partners across from each other. Each pair of players will need a softball with a strip of black electrical tape that cuts across all four of the seams. One partner starts with the striped ball in her throwing hand, using the proper grip across the seam with the middle finger on the tape and the thumb on the opposite side of the ball. Make sure players have plenty of room between the throwing players on either side for safety.

Execution
Players with a ball, using the proper grip, snap the striped ball to their partner. When using the proper grip, they can snap the striped ball to their partner while focusing on the rotation of the seams. Thrown with proper rotation, you will see a clean black line with the stripe. Players can make slight adjustments to their release to get the proper rotation. Players should snap the striped ball back and forth to one another 10 times.

Variations
To increase difficulty, have players stand farther apart. They can start at a distance of 8 feet and work their way to 10 or 15 feet (3 to 4.5 meters). They could grip the striped ball with their index finger on the top and their thumb on the bottom.

Coaching Points
Make sure the pads of the fingers are on the seams of the striped ball. Emphasize the snap of the wrist to create rotation and a clean, straight line with the tape on the ball. The wrist should be cocked back and snapping with a 12 o'clock to 6 o'clock rotation. Only the wrist should be used. For the variation grip, make sure players snap their wrist downward to create the proper spin. If the stripe on the ball is wobbly, the player is probably turning her wrist left or right.

45   ONE-KNEE THROWING

Purpose
To focus on throwing using the upper body parts

Organization
Position partners in two lines about 10 feet (3 meters) across from each other and about 5 feet (1.5 meters) from the players on either side.

Execution
Each pair throws the ball back and forth to each other from a position down on their throwing-side knee. Players should focus on transferring the ball from the glove to their hand and on executing a proper follow-through. Initially, have them do the drill with no ball, just going through the motions. They can work their way up to using a ball once they feel comfortable with the arm movements. You can break this drill down and have everyone with a ball working on transferring the ball to their throwing hand as quickly as they can.

Variations
Try the drill without gloves and using tennis balls. A weighted ball may be used at a distance of 10 feet (3 meters) or less.

Coaching Points
Make sure players are down on their throwing-side knee, which allows the hips and shoulders to rotate correctly. The elbow should be held at shoulder height. While transferring the ball, the throwing wrist should be cocked and the ball held in the finger pads (not in the palm.) When following through, the shoulders rotate in a downward fashion, and the throwing arm touches the opposite knee. As they continue to throw, players focus on the upper body, making sure they're rotating the throwing shoulder over the top. Have players elaborate on the follow-through by touching the ground with the throwing hand once the ball is released. The glove arm rotates downward with the elbow driving hard downward toward the glove-side hip. Make sure players understand the principle of using the glove hand. First have players throw using only their throwing arm; then progress to using the glove hand.

Purpose

To work on the throwing arm coming over the top rather than across the body

Organization

To help younger players understand this concept of accuracy, or throwing over the top down a straight line, put a bucket out in front of a coach 4 to 6 feet (1.2 to 2 meters) and form a line of outfielders in front of the bucket between 40 and 80 feet (12 to 24 meters), depending on their arm strength.

Execution

Players aim at the bucket and should attempt to throw the ball into the open end of the bucket that is facing them. Obviously it is important for outfielders to learn how to accurately throw a ball that will eventually bounce up to the target. In addition to outfielders, it is important for all players to work on their over-the-top mechanics for longer throws. The focus of this drill should be on the throwing arm coming over the top and not across the body.

Variations

You can use different size buckets for different levels of ability. Remove the bucket as players improve and their throws are in a straight line. You can substitute the bucket with another ball or a low profile cone. Younger athletes may need to start with a trash can versus a bucket.

Coaching Points

Emphasize that players use their legs. Throws should be accurate. The ball should go in a straight line rather than a rainbow arc. A rainbow throw takes longer to get to the play. Watch at which point players release the ball. If they release the ball too quickly, the ball will bounce too many times toward the bucket. If they release too late, the ball will sail over the bucket. The ball should bounce just as it is entering the bucket or actually could be thrown on a fly directly into the bucket. If using a cone or ball as the target in place of the bucket, then the object will be to hit the target with a direct throw.

47   LONG-HOP THROWS

Purpose
To work on accuracy

Organization
Position partners across from each other about 80 to 100 feet (24 to 30 meters) apart. For safety reasons, beginners should start with the ball on the same side; make sure there's ample room between sets of partners.

Execution
Players throw balls to their partner. They must allow the ball to bounce at least once before their partner is allowed to catch the ball. As the drill continues, have partners increase the distance between them. They continue to work on strengthening their arms and throws, as well as their accuracy.

Variations
Start beginners closer together and emphasize accuracy. Challenge advanced players in pairs by seeing which group can throw the farthest, which group has the best accuracy, which group can throw the farthest with the best accuracy, and which group can throw consistently with only one bounce. For another variation, you can place a receiving player sitting on a bucket so the ball has to bounce out in front and be accurate enough that the receiver does not need to stand up or move side to side to make the catch.

Coaching Points
First and foremost, make sure the ball bounces out in front of the partner and not at the partner's ankle. The player should be throwing long hops. Stress that when they're throwing the ball to a base for a tag play, the player at the base should be able to handle the long one-hop throw with ease. It's much easier to handle a bounce four to six feet (1.2 to 2 meters) out in front. Throws should be accurate and quick to the play. Throws should be in a straight line—no rainbow throws. Long hops are also good to use when the receiver is blinded from the sun or when an infielder is moving away from the base that she's trying to throw to.

Purpose

To work on front flips until they can be executed at game speed

Organization

Start with two lines of players about 10 to 12 feet (3 to 3.5 meters) across from one another.

Execution

The first player in line A begins by rolling a grounder to the first player in line B. As the player in line B moves forward to field the ball, she'll use a forward flip to toss the ball to the second player in line A. After the first player from line A rolls the grounder to the first player in line B, she sprints to the opposite line and get behind the last player in that line. The player who flips the ball to the player in the opposite line continues forward to take her place behind the last player in line A. Continue this process for each set of players.

Variations

This is a great drill to work on many variations of throwing as well as conditioning. You can use this drill inside or outside. If you have many players, form several groups (always allowing plenty of room between groups).

Coaching Points

When working on a forward flip, the ball should be in the fingertips and not the palm. Watch the point of the flip to ensure the throwing hand doesn't go back to go forward. The wrist should be cocked with fingers pointing back toward the fielder. Stress the follow-through of the hand movement to be out toward the target and not an upward motion.

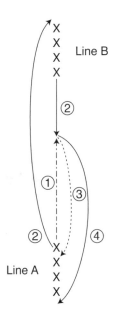

Purpose

To work on executing the backhand toss at game speed

Organization

Start with two lines about 10 to 12 feet (3 to 3.5 meters) across from one another.

Execution

The first player in line A rolls a grounder to the first player in line B.

As the player in line B moves forward to field the ball, she uses a drop step and tosses the ball to the second player in line B. (A drop step is a step back with the same foot as the throwing arm in the direction of the line being tossed to.) As players drop step, their throwing hand tosses the ball to the next player in line. After the first player from line A rolls a grounder to the first player in line B, she takes her place behind the last player in the same line. After a player flips the ball to another player, the first player rotates to the back of the line. Repeat the process for all players.

Variations

If you have many players, form several groups, allowing ample space between groups. To increase the drill's difficulty, increase distance between players.

Coaching Points

Run this drill inside or outside. When working on backhand tosses, the ball should be held in the pads of the fingers of the throwing hand. Watch the point of the toss, making sure the throwing hand moves toward the target. Stress the follow-through of the hand movement to be out toward the target, not in an upward motion. This movement should be short and quick. There's no backswing in the throwing arm.

Purpose

To work on running and tossing the ball accurately at full speed

Organization

Players work with partners about 15 to 20 feet (4.5 to 6 meters) across from one another.

Execution

The player in line A rolls a slow grounder to the player across from her in line B. The player in line B runs up to field the grounder and continues her run toward her partner in line A. Without stopping, the fielder throws the ball to her partner. Repeat 10 times.

Variations

Begin with one group at 1B and the other group at SS. The first player at 1B rolls a grounder to the first player at SS. The player at SS fields the grounder, continues to run toward 1B, and throws the ball. Once the player releases the ball, she sprints to the end of the opposite line at 1B. The player in line at 1B rolls a grounder to the next player in line at SS. Continue the drill until it's executed correctly. To decrease the degree of difficulty and to give players more repetitions, have them work in pairs instead of two lines.

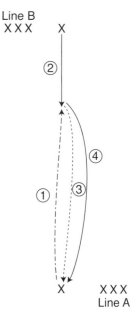

Coaching Points

You can run this drill inside or outside. This is an all-in-one drill that works on both throwing and conditioning. Stress the sprinting part of the drill. When sprinting toward the target, players should focus on a short and quick wrist-snap on the throw. Watch for players' throwing hands to be out in front of them with elbows about shoulder height. The release should resemble a dart throw. The wrist snaps back, and little arm movement occurs. The ball should be thrown sharply and straight toward the target. Reiterate that this is a quick and short throw in a straight line (like a dart throw), so there's little to no windup.

RELAY THROWS

Purpose
To work on communication and consistent throws between teammates

Organization
A group of four players in a line stand 15 to 20 feet (4.5 to 6 meters) apart. A player on one end starts with the ball.

Execution
Player 1 throws to player 2. Player 2 throws to player 3, and player 3 throws to player 4 (*a*). As the ball travels down the line, players 2 and 3 work on communicating with teammates as well as on their catching and receiving. The middle two players are in a ready position so that they can quickly throw the ball to the next player. In the ready position, the receiver's throwing side should be facing the thrower's glove side. The receiver will be standing in a nearly sideways stance. After the ball passes down the line several times, rotate player 1 with player 2 and player 3 with player 4. Basically, you're switching your interior players with your exterior players. This allows everyone to work on communication skills and relay throws.

Variations
Decrease the distance for beginning players. For advanced players, move player 4 behind player 1 (*b*). You'll now have only one player in the middle, and one side will have two players while the farther side has only one. When adding an extra player, this player will throw the ball to the inside player (player 2) and sprint to that spot. Player 2 will throw the ball to player 3 and then sprint to replace player 3.

Coaching Points
Players should throw first and then follow their throw. Players are constantly moving in this drill, so make sure each thrower, after she releases the ball, doesn't cut across in front of the next thrower. If players are stationary, make sure the middle two players are receiving and throwing the ball correctly.

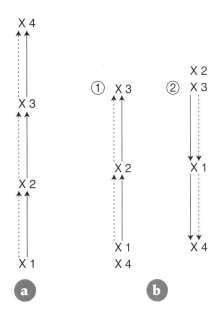

Purpose

To work on increasing the quickness of ball transfer from glove hand to throwing hand

Organization

Players work in partners facing each other about 10 to 12 feet (3 to 3.5 meters) apart. Make sure there's plenty of space between each pair.

Execution

Player A starts the drill by throwing the ball to her partner, player B. Player B steps toward the throw and works on catching and receiving mechanics. As she receives the ball, the transfer begins. This process consists of the glove hand rotating in toward the throwing shoulder in a quick fashion. As the rotation begins, the throwing hand reaches into the glove to grip the ball. The feet are moving toward the catch of the ball. The player with the ball moves quickly to release the ball back to her partner. The throwing arm is short with a quick release.

Variations

For beginners, move partners closer together. Challenge advanced players by giving them a set time (e.g., 30 seconds) to complete a certain amount of throws. For younger players or beginners, use tennis balls. If players have a hard time making the transfer, try the drill without gloves. This way you'll be able to tell what each player is doing wrong.

Coaching Points

When working with younger players or beginners, watch to make sure the transfer of the ball from glove hand to throwing hand is done correctly. Watch their shoulders for correct rotation. Make sure the feet are moving while the ball is being received. The non-throwing-side foot moves forward toward the target, and the throwing-side foot rotates with the glove hand during the transfer of the ball. Players tend to rush everything, and some will throw sidearm. They need to be quick with the transfer and the release.

FOUR-CORNER THROWS

Purpose

To work on accuracy, quickness of ball transfer, and footwork

Organization

Players line up four or five deep at each base.

Execution

Start the ball with the group at home plate. Home throws the ball to 1B, 1B throws to 2B, 2B throws to 3B, and 3B throws back home. After each player throws the ball, she goes to the end of the line. Feet are moving to allow the catch of the ball. Players work on releasing the ball quickly to the player at the next base. Make sure feet move in the direction of the next base.

Variations

This drill is to work on quickness and accuracy, so move beginning players closer together. Challenge advanced players by giving them a set time (30 seconds) to do the drill and complete 30 throws. For younger players or beginners, use tennis balls. For more advanced players, switch the direction after so many times around the bases.

Coaching Points

When working with younger players or beginners, make sure the transfer of the ball from glove hand to throwing hand is done correctly. Watch their feet, which should be moving as they receive the ball. The non-throwing-side foot moves forward toward the target, and the throwing-side foot rotates with the glove hand during the transfer of the ball. You'll notice that beginners tend to rush everything, and some will throw sidearm, which needs to be corrected.

Players need to be quick with the transfer and release. Make sure everyone is moving to catch the ball rather than standing and reaching, which slows down the throwing process.

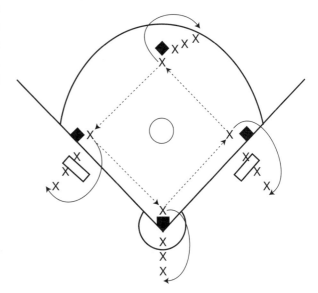

Purpose

To work on accuracy and concentration

Organization

Players line up at all infield positions except for the pitcher's position. Extra players take a place behind the players at these positions.

Execution

Start the ball with the group at home plate. Home throws the ball to the SS, SS throws to 1B, 1B throws to 3B, 3B throws to 2B, and 2B throws home. After each player throws the ball, she goes to the back of her line. Feet should be moving toward the catch of the ball. Players work on releasing the ball quickly to the player at the next base. Make sure their feet are moving in the direction of their target.

Variations

This drill is to work on quickness and accuracy, so move beginning players closer together. Challenge advanced players by giving them a set time (30 seconds) to do the drill and complete 30 throws. To make the drill harder for more advanced players, have them rotate in a circle toward their right. After a couple of times, have them rotate to the position toward their left. Use tennis balls for younger players or beginners.

Coaching Points

Make sure players are moving to catch the ball and aren't standing and reaching, which slows down the throwing process. Their feet should be moving in the direction of the target. When working with younger players or beginners, watch to make sure they're transferring the ball from glove hand to throwing hand correctly. The non-throwing-side foot moves forward toward the target, and the throwing-side foot rotates with the glove hand during the transfer of the ball. Make sure that the player is always stepping in the direction of the target with the glove foot.

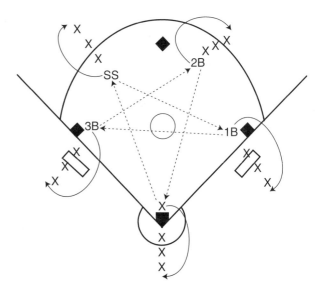

Chapter 5

Base Running

Jay Miller Mississippi State University Head Coach

Teams could win 15 to 20 percent more games each season if they could simply learn to run the bases well. Many teams in competition, even teams at the top level of division I, have some severe base-running weaknesses and lack proper base-running skills. Base running is a much overlooked and undervalued skill in softball. Proper base running can make a huge difference in your season if you're willing to make it a priority during practice.

Some basic rules exist that can set the foundation of your overall base-running philosophy. Following these rules can give you a great edge on your opponents. Take a look for yourself and try some of these principles with your team to see how they work for you. You'll find they lead to more runs for your team over the season.

1. Be aggressive at all times; go until you can go no further. Make the defense stop you each and every play. The more pressure you can put on your opponents, the more mistakes they'll make and the more rushed throws they'll have. This leads to extra bases and more runs for your team.

2. Run the bases to score every play. Tell your players there's no such thing as a single. Right from the first step out of the batter's box, you're trying to score, going as hard as possible until the defense stops you. As a runner you're looking to score every time the ball's put into play.

3. In all two-out situations, go two bases. Too many teams and players play this game base to base rather than pushing the defense into making a play to stop their runners. Tell your players never to be satisfied with one base. Always look to push the opponent.

4. Don't be afraid to run into outs. This is a coaching philosophy more than anything. If you're tentative with your players and get upset with them when they run into outs, you'll never develop the aggressiveness it takes to be a great base-running team. Sure, you'll get runners thrown out at times, but over the long season you'll score many more runs and win many more games by being aggressive.

5. Put your players in base-running situations every day in practice. Do most of your conditioning on the bases, and run game situations every time you take batting practice. This allows your players to read and react to the various situations they'll encounter in games. Run at game speed every play. Practicing this daily also helps your defense adjust and develop into pressure players.

This chapter includes some favorite drills for you to try with your team. Experiment and tweak these drills to fit your team and program, and you'll find that they help you score a few more runs this season.

55 PLOWS

Purpose
To work on developing an explosive start from the batter's box or off the base by building resistance and strength

Organization
Players pair off with waist bands. One player holds the band while the other places the band around her waist. Pairs line up on a foul line with cones placed about 60 feet (18 meters) away.

Execution
On command (whistle or clap), the player wearing the waist band runs toward the cones 60 feet away while her partner provides resistance by holding the band. When the first runner reaches the cones, partners switch roles and come back to the foul line.

Variation
Rather than use bands, players can simply hold their partner's shoulders as they drive off the base. Hold for about 10 feet (3 meters), then release and sprint to the cones.

Coaching Point
Pair players up according to ability for this drill.

Purpose

To help develop an explosive start from the batter's box or off the base; to work on acceleration

Organization

Players pair off with rubber tubing and belts. Players place belts around their waist and stretch the tubing out between them. Pairs line up on a foul line with cones placed about 100 feet (30.5 meters) away.

Execution

On command (whistle or clap), the player in front begins to run while the player in back remains standing in place. When the tubing is stretched twice its length, the back runner takes off. When they reach the cones, partners switch and come back to the foul line.

Variation

You can vary the amount of stretch you have on the tubing, depending on how fast your players are and how much you want to push them.

Coaching Points

Watch for proper running form, especially for the back runners. Check the bands for wear every day before use. When they begin to show wear, replace them with new tubing to prevent them from breaking and snapping your players.

Purpose
To warm up before practice

Organization
All players meet with the coach at home plate. This is a great time to talk briefly to your team about the day's practice or any other item of interest. After discussion, the players warm up by jogging around the bases.

Execution
Rather than jogging around the field, have your players jog around the bases, working on proper turns at each base and accelerating through each turn. Proper running form is important; hitting the base in the perfect spot is required or the player should start again at home. Vary the number of laps (home to home), running 5 to 10 laps on average. Following the laps, go into your stretching and dynamic warm-up routine to begin practice.

Coaching Point
You can begin every team practice with a jog or slow running warm-up. This creates a clear routine for the start of practice.

Purpose

To reduce base-running times and monitor progress of your team

Organization

All players line up at home plate. Take three basic times each week:

Home to 1B: 3 to 5 chances

2B to home: 2 or 3 chances

Home to home: 1 or 2 chances

Execution

Time from a standing start at home plate with one foot on home plate and the other foot back behind the plate. The stopwatch starts when the foot leaves home and stops again when the foot touches the base. This provides a consistent measure of running speed.

You can time any bases in any order. The key is to be consistent and time regularly. Some weeks you might only time one chance; other times you might take a bit longer and give each player three to five chances.

Variations

Set up cones at the following intervals between home and 1B: 5 yards (4.5 meters), 10 yards (9 meters), and 20 yards (18 meters). Execute the drill as normal. One person stands at each cone with a stopwatch and times the runner as she passes. This gives you a clear sense of what each player needs to work on: her start, her finish, or her overall speed through the length of the run.

Another variation is to use the time from bat contact to first base; comparing this time to the straight running time gives you an idea of who needs to work on getting out of the box.

Coaching Points

Do this drill at the beginning of practice, after warm-up when players are fresh. You can then repeat the drill at the end of practice, after they're tired, and compare their times. Who can reach their times when fatigued? Have your players try to reach personal bests when they run.

59   ONE BASE

Purpose
To work on getting a lot of sprints in a short amount of time

Organization
Split your team into four groups; each group lines up at one base, including home.

Execution
Coach signals "go!" and the first runner at each base sprints to the next base. As soon as the player crosses the base, the next runner in line takes off (e.g., when the runner from home reaches 1B, the next person in line at 1B takes off for 2B.) This gives you four runners running at a time with little rest for each runner between sprints. Have your players time their take-off to be as soon as the runner passes in front of them. You don't want your players waiting too long after the front runner has passed the base. Do this drill for about five minutes.

Variation
Have each player run two bases (or more) rather than one. This makes for longer sprints and helps players work on making good turns.

Coaching Points
You can vary the time depending on your goals for the day: extra conditioning, reward for good work, and so on. Make sure your players are sprinting hard through the base and not slowing up until they're past it. You want maximum effort on each sprint. You might try to see how long your team can go with maximum effort by timing them and using that time as a baseline for future drills.

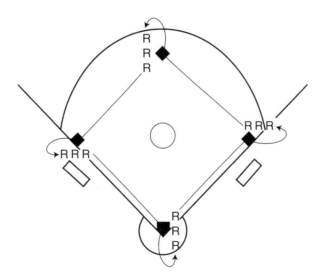

Purpose

To motivate players to keep their place in line or to move up to the front (fastest); to get maximum effort on each and every sprint

Organization

Have players line up on a foul line in the order of their running speed from home to first (fastest to slowest). Place cones 60 feet (18.2 meters) away to indicate a finish line.

Execution

On command (whistle or clap), everyone sprints through the cones 60 feet away. The goal is to make sure you don't get beat by the person to your slow side. If you get beat by a slower runner, you must run again (sprint by yourself). You can run this drill for a set number of repetitions or until you observe that everyone is working hard and giving maximum effort.

Variation

Change the order of your players and see if they can challenge to move up in line. The goal is to work your way up the line as far as possible toward the fastest player.

Coaching Points

This drill provides some competition while running sprints and is a great way to get everyone running hard. Watch for all players running hard each and every sprint. Players should be working hard to improve their times.

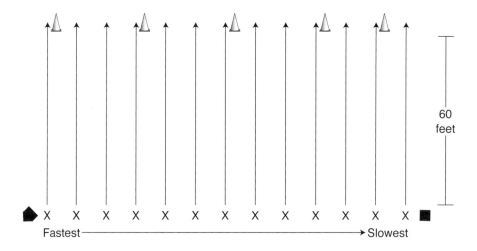

Purpose

To work on players' timing in taking leads off the pitcher and returning to the base to avoid tags

Organization

Break your team up into three groups, with one group at each base (not counting home plate). A coach or pitcher on the rubber goes through a pitching motion or actually pitches a ball.

Execution

One runner at each base assumes a leadoff stance. The pitcher throws the ball or goes through her pitching motion, and each runner works on her timing; she tries to get off the base as soon as the ball is released. Runners take a two- or three-step lead and then stop and return to the base, working on avoiding a tag by the next player who steps up and simulates a tag. Runners proceed to the next base, and the next player in line steps up and assumes her leadoff stance for the next pitch.

Variations

Use this drill in three stages. First run the drill just as described with leads and returns to the base. At the next stage work on straight steals; runners get their jump and run straight through the next base. At the third stage work on hit-and-run execution, where runners "sneak a peek" toward home plate about two to three steps off base and round the next base. Make sure your players turn only their head to take a look at the batter. Turning their shoulders slows them down and hurts their chances of stealing the base.

Coaching Points

Videotaping your players' leads is a great teaching tool. Place a video camera in foul ground to the side of first to capture runners at 1B and 3B, along with the pitcher on the rubber. Let the camera run during the drill and take a look to see who leaves early or late. Have the coach or pitcher actually throw a ball to give you a better frame of reference. Showing your team the video the next day (or on a rainy day) is fun and educational.

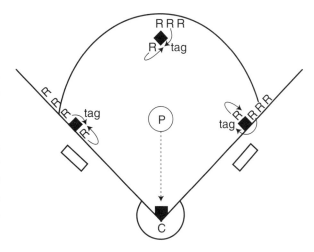

Purpose

To work on correctly hitting the bases and making correct turns around the bases

Organization

All players start at home plate and line up ready to run the bases.

Execution

The first player runs from home to 1B. After the first player touches 1B, the next in line runs to 1B, and all others subsequently follow one at a time. The players then return to the line at home plate following their turn. After all players have run four times to 1B, they run three times to 2B, two times to 3B, and a final time home to home, returning to the line at home plate between each turn.

Variations

You can reverse the action (1-2-3-4) or add additional runs, such as 4-3-2-1-2-3-4. You can also have double days (8-6-4-2) or make other changes, such as 10-1-1-1 or other variations.

Coaching Points

Be as strict as you like with the execution of this drill. The goal is perfection. All players must hit the base perfectly or the drill starts over. Make sure players accelerate through the base, square up after they hit 1B, hit the front outside corner when running through 1B, and hit the inside corner perfectly on turns.

63 CLAP AND GO

Purpose
To practice making quick adjustments after a slide

Organization
Split your team into four groups; one group lines up at each base. At each base, the first player in line assumes a position as described:

Home: Lie down face first with head toward 1B.

1B: Sit upright on the base facing 2B with feet straight out.

2B: Lie down on back with head on base and feet toward 1B.

3B: Sit down facing the outfield with feet straight out toward the left-field line.

Execution
A coach is at the pitching rubber and claps or blows a whistle. On this signal, the players get up and run as fast as they can to the next base. The next player in line then assumes the correct position, and the coach blows the whistle again. Do this drill for about 10 minutes.

Variations
Use various positions at each base; change these around each time you do this drill. You can position players in many ways, so be creative.

Coaching Points
This drill is fun, provides good conditioning for base running, and is a great drill to end practice with. You can vary the time you spend depending on your goals for the day: extra conditioning, reward for good work, and so on.

Purpose
To work on proper base running and getting good jumps

Organization
Split your team into four groups; each group lines up at a base. Place a coach or pitcher on the mound to go through the throwing motion.

Execution
On the pitch, the first runner at each base runs around to home (e.g., the runner at 3B runs to home, the runner at 2B runs to 3B and then to home, and so on). After everyone reaches home, the next players in line do the same on the next pitch. When a player reaches home, she walks to the next base (e.g., if she began at 1B, she goes to 2B and gets in line there). All players returning to where they started equals one round.

Variations
Vary the number of rounds depending on how much conditioning the players need. You might also start over for poor jumps, missed bases, and the like.

Coaching Points
This is a good drill to get your players in the mindset that they're always trying to score. Have a coach monitor players' jumps to make sure they're leaving at the correct time in relation to the pitch. It is recommended that players take off when the pitcher's arm is about halfway down from the top of her circle. This gives the player the best jump without being called for leaving too early. Players should work on proper turns at each base. You can place coaches on the bases to work on their coaching signals. Runners practice reading coaching signals for slides, turning on the base, and taking the bases ahead.

65   **TWO AT A TIME**

Purpose

To work on proper base running and getting good jumps; to work on coach and runner communication

Organization

All players line up at home plate. Place a coach or pitcher on the mound to go through the throwing motion. Have a coach at 1B and 3B to direct runners.

Execution

On the pitch, the first two runners from home take off. The first runner runs through 1B, while the second runner rounds 1B and heads to 2B. Coaches now communicate to the runner what they want the runner to do: bring the second runner to 3B or home, stop at 2B, and so on. When runners have stopped, the pitcher goes through her motion again, and the runners work on their jumps and score. They then join the line at home plate to wait for their next turn. The next two runners start at home and do the same as the first two.

Variation

If your players need sliding work, add a slide as they arrive at 2B, 3B, and home.

Coaching Points

This is one of the best drills for working on signals and communication. Both verbal and physical signals should be used and practiced during this drill to prepare players for communicating in game situations.

Purpose

To train athletes how and when to tag up on fly balls

Organization

Divide your team into three groups. Place a group at each base: 1B, 2B, and 3B. You'll need a coach at home plate with a bucket of balls and a bat. You'll also need at least one coach, manager, or player in the outfield but preferably a fielder in each of the outfield positions.

Execution

The first player at each base should be standing in her lead position. As the coach hits a fly ball to the outfield or foul territory, each player either tags up or leads off, depending on the base and the hit. The coach should clearly define to their runners what they expect at each base prior to starting the drill. This helps a coach to evaluate a player's decision on why she would either tag up or come off as far as she can. As each player correctly tags up and advances, she moves forward to the next base and gets in the back of the line. The next person in each line then takes her spot in the leadoff position before the coach hits the next fly ball.

Variations

If you put a pitcher on the mound and a catcher behind the plate, you can have each player time her leadoff with the pitcher's release; then the coach will hit the ball so that the timing is gamelike and the players can react. When trying this variation, the coach may mix in occasional ground balls that the runners need to aggressively advance on without tagging up.

Coaching Points

Make sure players use proper technique on their tag-up positions and get the best possible jumps. Players should also be encouraged to tag up only on balls that they'll advance on if the catch is made. If they would not normally advance if the catch is made, then they should not tag up but should come off the base as far as they safely can in case the ball falls. Of course they want to avoid being in jeopardy of being doubled off if the catch is made. All players need to understand that they should always tag up on all foul balls, regardless of the distance from the base. They will never need to come off and read the ball when the ball is clearly foul.

Chapter 6

Hitting

Jennifer Ogee University of Nebraska Assistant Coach

Hitting is considered one of the most difficult skills in the game of softball. The speed of the pitch, the spin of the ball, the hitter's ability to process the correct information and respond in less than half a second—all these factors contribute to the complexity and difficulty of the offensive game. Hitting is crucial in softball because a win or a loss is ultimately determined by each team's offensive production. Many hitters view total offensive production in terms of whether or not they get a hit. A good hitter is one who is successful getting hits "only" 30 percent of the time. But being a *great* hitter isn't just about success with the bat every third time up to the plate. Much more is involved in being a winning hitter than just putting the bat on the ball. Hitting is about having a clear mind and the ability to visualize success and be consistent. The mental part of being a successful hitter is so important and yet not frequently discussed.

Hitting is a visual skill. Regardless of the type of swing she uses, if a hitter doesn't see the ball well, she can't hit it. Part of "seeing" is believing in the work you have done and in the game you are capable of playing. A hitter who trusts in her preparation enhances her confidence and consistency. Every hitter will experience ups and downs; one day fans roar their approval, and the next they yell catcalls. There will be days when the best hitter feels defeated, and climbing out of the valleys will take a great deal of strength and courage. Though easier said than done, being consistent in her work, controlling her thoughts, and being accountable for those can help a player more quickly regain a clear focus and renewed confidence. Even in the hardest times, she has to visualize success. There's nothing like breaking out of a slump to rekindle your confidence and competitive energy, but it takes work.

How does a player become a consistent hitter with a sustained level of self-confidence? Ironically, it's not always through a track record of success at the plate. A friend of mine often said, "You've got to understand that there are things you can control and things you just can't." A hitter can't totally control the number of hits she gets or the outcome of her at-bat, but she *can* control how she responds to that outcome. Skills are important, but along with skills a hitter must have an internal drive to be the best she can be. This starts with knowing everything she can about herself as a hitter. What are her natural strengths and weaknesses? Does she have the internal drive to be the best she can be? Is she a student of the game? What kind of attitude does she maintain? Does she have a plan in her workouts and at the plate? Does she understand the fundamentals of the swing? Does she practice like she plays, with focus and purpose? Developing self-awareness helps the hitter make an informed response to her performance based on an honest appraisal of the type of hitter she is. It also helps her coaches to help her with appropriate improvement plans. Being diligent about those plans not only helps to correct and strengthen skills but strengthens the mental game as well. A hitter who has the requisite physical skills, sharp focus, and can visualize success, even when the hits aren't coming, will be perceived as an offensive threat.

When a hitter understands how she plays, an appropriate plan can be developed to improve her game. At this juncture, a coach can introduce techniques and tools to improve the hitter's fundamentals and create a personal hitting strategy to guide her through her career. Great coaches take the lead as strategists, helping to reinforce good practices and correct bad habits, but most important, they help their players to see themselves as the hitters they can be and help them to get there, physically and mentally. While a coach helps a player make physical adjustments and corrections, he or she can also help her adjust in attitude, work ethic, and confidence. A great hitting coach, although not ultimately responsible for a hitter's results, can certainly facilitate the hitter's rise out of a slump. If the hitting coach doesn't show confidence in the hitter, how is the hitter to rekindle her self-confidence? Many a hitter has failed to climb out of a slump at least partly because her own hitting coach's frustration belittled her and eroded what little confidence she had.

Good coaches maintain a consistent approach to practice, not simply reinforcing fundamentals but applauding the outcome as well. A hitter will sense when a coach is offering false praise; likewise, she'll appreciate and respond to well-earned praise. Positive reinforcement is a powerful tool. Practice is required not only to produce improvement but to maintain consistency in basic skills. Drills can be remedial in helping to fix a problem, and they also reinforce consistency. Practice might not make a batter perfect, but it will surely advance her progress in that direction. Remember that good hitting coaches do more than remediation; their goal is to develop consistent hitters and confident players.

You can break down hitting and analyze the swing in many ways. This chapter focuses on the development of good physical practice habits along with good mental habits. These drills are particularly helpful in establishing a sound foundation in terms of physical skills and habits as well as mental discipline and consistency. Each drill has its own purpose. Taken as a whole, they're designed to establish good habits and consistency while reinforcing discipline and mental toughness. The drills should be executed often and in a disciplined manner until perfect execution becomes nearly automatic. Don't underplay the role of the coach in this process. A great coach can contribute much to developing willing players into consistent hitters and confident players. Coaches, as you work with your players to develop their game, may you have patience, confidence in your own ability, and the luck of the perfect pitch.

Purpose

To warm up hitters' swings and reinforce good hitting fundamentals while maintaining a good athletic position throughout the swing

Organization

You need a bat and a plate for each batter.

Execution

The hitter assumes a hitter's stance in the batter's box. The hitter visualizes different pitches and practices gamelike swings to all nine contact points of the strike zone. Hold the finished swing for a count of two to create muscle memory and body awareness.

Variations

A coach or hitting partner may stand in as the pitcher and go through their entire windup and call out the location of the pitch to the hitter. The hitter can use a lighter bat to train bat speed or a heavier bat to train strength.

Coaching Point

Hitters should go through the entire sequence of their swing, maintaining balance throughout.

Purpose

To work on a hitter's ability to see and feel her muscles working the correct fundamentals of the swing; to practice the different segments of the swing (stance, load, stride to swing)

Organization

You'll need a bat and a mirror for each batter. Place the mirror in front of the hitter as if she's looking at the pitcher, or put it in the opposite batter's box.

Execution

The hitter assumes a hitter's stance. Break her swing down into segments: stance, load, stride, and swing. She should hold each segment for two seconds to build muscle memory.

Coaching Points

Many times hitters don't have the body awareness to make certain adjustments. Coaches can tell a hitter to get to a strong launching position, but what does that look like in the hitter's eyes? Seeing is believing.

Purpose

To keep weight on the inside half of the back leg and prevent hitters from drifting

Organization

Hitters stand on a baseball pitcher's mound or the side of a hill so that they're on an incline.

Execution

Each batter assumes a hitter's stance on the incline (her front foot will be going uphill). She practices taking stride and getting to a strong launching position while keeping her weight loaded and balanced. She should move from stance to stride and then repeat to gain proper muscle memory.

Variation

Hitters can re-create this drill on a flat surface by standing in on pitchers as they are working out and focusing on their timing and rhythm; weight should be maintained on the inside of the back leg.

Coaching Points

Hitters get a better understanding and feel for what it means when you say, "Stay back." Make sure hitters keep their weight on the inside half of their back leg.

Purpose

To reinforce proper hitting mechanics to different parts of the zone

Organization

This drill requires a tee, a ball, and a separate plate for each batter. Or have hitters take turns. Use the plate to represent home plate. Position the tee to simulate a specific type of pitch and location of the ball. Adjust the tee so that the hitter is at her correct point of contact.

Execution

The hitter assumes her stance with both eyes looking out at the pitcher. She should work on getting to a balanced launching position, a strong contact point, and lengthening her swing through contact to extension and follow-through.

Variations

Have a pitcher go through her entire windup so a hitter can work her full timing of swing, while keeping the drill as close to gamelike as possible. You might also have a specific target at which the ball should be hit. Challenge your hitters to hit that target. Make a game of it.

Coaching Points

The hitter needs to understand the different contact points for an outside pitch versus a middle or inside pitch. Routinely alter the tee's height and location. Make this drill as gamelike as possible. By making a game of it, you take out the "paralysis by analysis" and add competition to the drill.

Purpose

To take the forward stride temporarily out of the swing to help facilitate a proper load to the back side while hitting against a firm front side

Organization

You'll need a tee, a bat, and a ball for each batter.

Execution

The hitter assumes a narrow hitting stance with feet less than shoulder width apart. She grips the bat directly in front of the middle of her chest. The barrel of the bat should be pointed directly up toward the sky (*a*). She takes a step toward the catcher with her back foot into a strong launching position with both feet and hands (*b*). Weight transfers into a firm front side as she initiates her swing.

Coaching Point

This is a great drill to reinforce the sequence of the swing and hitting into a firm front side.

Purpose
To create a "feel" for hitters for proper weight shift and momentum through the ball

Organization
You'll need a ball, a bat, and a tee for each batter.

Execution
The hitter assumes a narrow stance outside and back of the batter's box. Her belly button faces the ball and tee. Her hands start in the middle of her body, perpendicular to the ground and at the top of her strike zone. She takes a crossover step toward the tee with her back foot while her hands naturally drive the bat against her back shoulder (a). She lifts her front knee up toward her back knee, allowing her weight to transfer back. Her stride foot comes forward to a strong launching position, and she swings (b).

Coaching Point
This drill should help create proper momentum and timing to execute proper weight transfer.

Purpose
To reinforce the proper sequence of the swing; to improve eye–hand coordination

Organization
You'll need a bat and a ball for each batter.

Execution
The batter assumes her hitting stance and then loads and strides to a strong launching position. She tosses the ball to the appropriate zone *(a)*. If the toss is a ball, she takes the pitch *(b)*. If the toss is a strike, she hits a hard line drive into the outfield.

Variation
To simulate different pitches, have hitters alter the height and location of the toss.

Coaching Points
Throughout this drill it's important for the hitter to feel the proper weight shift and sequence of the swing. She should also focus on keeping her chest on the ball. Note that the way a hitter takes a pitch is just as important as her swing. Striding forward is important on all pitches, but if she takes the pitch, she will maintain a neutral position and not rotate.

Purpose

To reinforce keeping the hands inside the ball and keeping the barrel head in the hitting zone for an extended period of time

Organization

You'll need a hitting screen, a cone, an open field, a bucket of balls, and a bat. A coach tosses to hitters. The coach stands behind a hitting screen set up on the hitter's opposite-side foul line (on 1B foul line for right-handed hitters). Place the cone on the pitcher's mound to simulate the pitcher.

Execution

The hitter assumes her hitting stance in the batter's box about 15 to 20 feet (4.5 to 6 meters) away from the screen. The coach tosses the ball. Hitters time the pitch and swing.

Coaching Point

The hitter might lose a little power in this drill but will gain quickness and a keener sense for proper bat path.

Purpose

To help hitters develop a proper swing while adjusting to different pitches throughout the strike zone

Organization

You'll need a hitting screen, an open field, a bucket of balls, and a bat. A coach stands behind a hitting screen set up 20 feet (6 meters) in front of the pitcher's mound.

Execution

The hitter assumes her hitting stance in the batter's box. As the coach starts the underhand motion back, the hitter begins her load and motion back. The toss will be underhand. The hitter stays through the correct plane of the pitch for an extended period of time while creating bat speed through the hitting zone.

Coaching Points

This is a great drill to simulate live pitching. Coaches can control exactly where they want the ball to go in the strike zone. Be sure to fake a toss every now and then to keep the hitter honest in making sure she's staying back and reacting to the pitch.

Purpose

To create a feel for the bottom hand setting the plane of the swing and lengthening the hitting zone

Organization

You'll need a hitting screen, an open field, a bucket of balls, and a bat. The coach stands behind a hitting screen set up 20 feet (6 meters) in front of the pitcher's mound.

Execution

The hitter takes a normal grip on the bat except that her top hand is slightly open *(a)*. She assumes a hitting stance in the batter's box. After contact, the hitter releases her top hand and finishes the swing with her top hand pointing at the pitcher *(b)*.

Variation

Hitters can perform this drill off a tee, side toss, front toss, or live.

Coaching Point

Hitters should get immediate feedback on their increased bat speed and on how long the barrel of the bat was in the hitting zone.

77   DRIVE THE TUNNEL

Purpose
To increase each hitter's hand and arm strength through the ball and the hitting zone

Organization
This drill requires weighted balls, a batting cage (or an open field), and a bat. The drill can be executed off of a tee, soft toss, or front toss.

Execution
Set a target to indicate where the ball should be hit. You can use a net, a cone, a trash can, a bucket, or any other item that will not be damaged if hit by the batted ball. The farther the target is placed from the hitter, the more challenging the drill. The hitter assumes a hitter's stance and drives the ball the length of the cage (or into the open field).

Variations
Various sizes of weighted balls are available to enhance awareness of the bat path and plane of the ball. Also as mentioned, placing the target farther from the hitter can add to the difficultly.

Coaching Points
This drill is a great teacher for most hitters. Hitters get immediate feedback on their swing. This is a great training tool for warm-up or before games. This drill also trains a hitter's eye–hand coordination and sense of feel.

Purpose
To help hitters drive the ball to the opposite field

Organization
You'll need a bucket of balls, a screen, and an open field; this drill can be done off a front toss or live. Hitters take turns.

Execution
Establish a set number of pitches in each round. The hitter assumes her stance, and the ball is pitched to the middle to outside half of the plate. The hitter takes an aggressive gamelike swing through the inside half of the ball. If the hitter pops up or pulls the ball, the hitter's round is done.

Coaching Points
The goal is to drive the ball to the opposite half of the field without popping up or pulling the ball. This is a great drill to reinforce proper contact points and keeping the hands inside the ball. It's a self-coaching drill.

Purpose

To promote hitters going to the plate with a plan but realizing that plan might change

Organization

This drill is best performed off of live batting practice.

Execution

The coach establishes the number of outs per round and the scenario (e.g., four rounds of five pitched balls). In the first round, the hitter must execute one squeeze bunt, one hit and run, one sacrifice fly, one line drive, and one at-bat with two strikes.

Coaching Point

This drill helps hitters learn which pitch and swing pattern will best assist them in their executions.

Purpose
To work on the timing element of the swing, recognize different grips, and gain an understanding of different pitch types, including curveballs, screwballs, rise balls, drops, change-ups, and drop curves

Organization
You will need a pitcher, a catcher, a hitter, a helmet, and a plate.

Execution
The hitter assumes her stance in the batter's box. As the pitcher releases the pitch, the hitter works on the timing element of the swing *without* swinging. The hitter then calls out the pitch and the location.

Coaching Points
At the end of a pitcher's workout the pitcher tends to mix her pitches, so this is the best time for a hitter to stand in to bat. This is a great drill for hitters to develop knowledge of the strike zone; identify pitch, location, and grips; and build confidence in their swing. The manner in which a hitter takes a pitch is just as important as her swing. These two elements go hand in hand. Make sure the hitter is on time with the stride so that she can take in information from the pitcher to make a sound decision. It's essential that the hitter not swing.

81   LIVE PITCHING, HEAD TO HEAD

Purpose
To give hitters gamelike at-bats, focusing on the approach to the plate, timing, pitch recognition, and swing

Organization
You'll need a pitcher, a catcher, a helmet, a bat and ball, and a screen.

Execution
This drill can be performed in several different ways. One scenario is more like batting practice with the batter hitting multiple rounds. The coach establishes the number of balls the hitter will receive per round (e.g., three rounds of six pitches). Another scenario is to create the most gamelike situations as possible for the hitter. The battery will compete against the offense in a series of at-bats. This can be executed in a batting cage or open field.

Variations
Create scenarios for the hitter, such as runner at 2B, 1 out, 2-1 count. Have some fun with this by creating teams: the offense versus the battery and the umpire.

Coaching Points
Hitting off a live pitcher is as close to gamelike as a hitter can get. This helps build discipline and knowledge of the strike zone and hitting zone. It's crucial that the hitter works her entire approach as well as timing, pitch recognition, and swing. The hitter's approach includes the process of moving from the dugout to the on-deck circle and to the plate. The at-bat begins in the dugout, where the batter observes the pitcher's tendencies and tries to determine the pitcher's strengths and weaknesses and her "go to" pitch. While on deck, the hitter should focus on getting her timing down with the pitcher, practice game-like swings, and anticipate possible game situations. As the hitter walks to the plate, she should evaluate the situation and create a plan of attack. In the batter's box, she sees the ball and reacts. The game is on! It's important for hitters to realize that every at-bat is a privilege, and they must take advantage.

Bunting

Michelle Gromacki   Cal State Fullerton Head Coach

This chapter covers the techniques and importance of the sacrifice bunt, as well as other types of bunts similar to the sacrifice but which are generally used in very specific offensive situations. These bunts include the right-handed slap bunt, push bunt, squeeze bunt, and drag bunt (also called the sneaky bunt). The one type of bunt not covered here is the left-handed slap bunt, which is much different from slap bunting from the right side. This bunt is the subject of chapter 8.

It is a coach's job to make sure that young athletes understand the bigger picture of what they're trying to achieve physically. If they understand what role bunting plays in softball, they're more likely to be willing to put time into learning to bunt correctly. It's a coach's job to take them through the process of learning the skill so that they can then build on their mastery of the skill. Too few coaches establish the fundamental building blocks of learning a skill, especially one as mundane as bunting can be, and might skip the process. The drills in this chapter are intended to teach bunting one skill at a time.

Why is bunting so important? Bunting gets the bat on the ball when your team is having trouble making contact with a challenging pitcher. A bunt provides an avenue to create offensive pressure for a team that might be a bit weak offensively. Bunting can help generate base runners, move base runners into scoring position, and score base runners. Most coaches will tell you that any player should be able to bunt because bunting is easier than hitting. If you know the proper mechanics and have practiced them enough to be able to execute them in a game, and especially against tough pitching, then that statement is true. This section addresses each type of bunt and how it can be used in the game of softball.

First is the sacrifice bunt, the most basic short-game element of fastpitch softball. Batters use this bunt to sacrifice themselves as an out in order to advance a runner or runners into scoring position. To ensure that the bunt is laid down correctly, the batter usually turns and gets into bunting position early, which gives away her intentions of bunting. Making an out at first is not a concern, although the batter should always run out her bunt in case of an errant throw.

The sacrifice bunt is used only when there are fewer than two outs. The most common situations for sacrifice bunts are these: no outs and a runner on first base, a runner on second with no outs, or runners on first and second with no outs. There are also times when a coach chooses to give up a second out to put more pressure on a defense or a pitcher in a close game; this is most likely to occur in the later innings. In most cases, a bunting batter will have fewer than two strikes on her in the count. Earlier in a game, the sacrifice bunt can be used to read the defense and set up game strategy. If a team has a power hitter in the lineup coming up (preferably on deck or in the hole), a sacrifice bunt is often the best way to move runners into scoring position.

Similar to but different from the sacrifice bunt is the right-handed slap bunt. A successful slap bunt will fool the defense into believing that the batter is going to put down a sacrifice bunt. As the ball leaves the pitcher's hands, the bunter then pulls the bat back and puts her hands into a position to "slap" the ball past the charging corners into the alleys toward second base or shortstop. Coaches will most likely use the slap in the same situations as the sacrifice bunt. In some situations it becomes obvious that a slap might be more successful than a sacrifice. For example, a slap might be preferable when you have a very aggressive defensive team that's adept in moving the corners in to cut off the ball and getting the lead runner out in sacrifice situations. You might also notice some teams' middle infielders will leave their positions early in the sacrifice situation, which will create a hole in the defense. In such a case, a slap might not only advance the lead runner but also allow the batter to be safe at first base. The timing of the slap bunt is very important in order to sell it to the defense. Some teams use the slap when they're having little to no success off a pitcher, just to get the bat on the ball.

The push bunt is similar to the slap bunt in that it attempts to get a similar reaction from the defense. The only difference is that the push is slightly less aggressive; there might be no "chop" on the ball and more of a push of the bat and the entire body. You'll more likely see this bunt placed to the right side of the field when you have a weak fielding pitcher or a second baseman who vacates her position early. You must have a batter who can execute the push properly, preferably in the alley on the right side of the field.

The drag bunt (also called a sneaky bunt or a bunt for a base hit) is typically used as a means for the batter to reach first base safely. What makes this bunt successful, or not, is its placement and the batter's ability to deaden the ball, which puts the pressure on the defense to make fast and accurate throws or else get beat by the runner. You sometimes see power hitters put down the drag bunt as well because most defenses are caught off guard by a slugger trying to bunt. The drag is also used in situations with a very aggressive defense to surprise the defense in a sacrifice situation or in a situation with runners on with one or two outs. With hitters with a lot of speed, the drag can force throwing errors and allow runners to advance.

Finally, the squeeze bunt, or suicide bunt, is used with a runner on third base and fewer than two outs. This bunt can also be used with multiple runners on board when a team has had little success with runners in scoring position. A squeeze bunt requires the hitter to bunt the ball whether the pitch is a strike or a ball. The hitter must attempt to get the bunt down, knowing that the runner is taking off from third base as soon as the ball is released from the pitcher's hand. The hitter must at least make contact with the ball to protect the runner. Ideally, of course, the bunt is laid down, and the runner comes in to score from third base. In this play, called a "squeeze play," timing is crucial. If either the runner or the hitter makes a mistake, the play is botched, and a runner who was in scoring position is out. If the coach knows his or her personnel and is smart about when he or she calls it, the squeeze bunt is an effective way to score a run, especially when a team is having difficulty getting runners home.

Some of the drills that follow are specific to one kind of bunt; others can be used for them all. This information is given for each drill. Because you need to start with a foundation for successful bunting, the first drills are fundamental. They get more intricate as they progress. Players who understand that bunting and winning go hand in hand will have more success. Smart teams understand that each game is a battle and that you need as many weapons as possible to win, including effective bunting.

Purpose

To work on understanding the fundamentals of the sacrifice bunt and the timing of the turn off of the pitcher's windup

Organization

All players start in a basic hitting stance and spread out away from each other. They will be facing a mock pitcher (the coach). Best positioning is to have players located on the field and the pitcher standing at home plate facing all of the players. That setup gives bunters more room to move. If you have enough home plates (use gloves if necessary), throw one down next to every bunter.

Execution

Players begin in proper batting stance facing the pitcher. The pitcher simulates an entire pitching motion, and players turn at the correct time. If the timing is off, the coach corrects them. Once players turn, they are to freeze and hold their positions so the coaching staff can check their bunting positions, correcting as needed. This gives players a clearer sense of what they're doing wrong and how to fix it.

Variation

This same setup can be done for repetition of other types of bunts as well, including the slap bunt, push bunt, drag, and squeeze. Focusing on one type of bunt at a time allows coaches to give bunters great feedback on proper timing and movement.

Coaching Points

The proper timing of the turn is after the pitcher presents the ball and begins to push off the mound into her windup. In addition to the timing of the turn, proper form and technique can be viewed when the player freezes in bunting position. Coaches use this drill to work on timing as well as proper bunting form. Watch for proper plate coverage with the barrel of the bat. Bunters should be completely squared up and facing the pitcher with toes, knees, hips, and both shoulders. A relaxed, knee-bent position keeps the bat in the strike zone once the player has pivoted. With a variation of a different type of bunt, the timing element specific to the bunt type can be emphasized in repetition and with several bunters at once.

Purpose

To work on sacrifice bunting fast-moving pitches

Organization

Place a pitching machine in a cage or on the field with a bucket of balls nearby. You'll need a home plate, a batting helmet, and a bat. To make this drill as gamelike as possible, place the pitching machine at proper distance from home. (The machine should not be on top of the pitching rubber but near the release point that most pitchers would get to in front of the mound.)

Execution

The coach or player feeding the machine should hold the ball up while the bunter is in her batting stance. Bunters should square around as the feeder drops a hand toward the machine. The bunter works on executing sacrifice bunts. She should square around for each pitch to practice proper timing. If bunters are feeling rushed, they should step out of the box and get back in when they're ready.

Variations

You can add many challenges to this drill. Place cones in a semicircle about 10 to 12 feet (3 to 3.5 meters) in front of the plate to work on soft hands. The bunter attempts to keep the ball inside of the cones to soften her bunts. Use the same cones to work on directional bunting. Put two machines side by side, one set much slower than the first, and have your feeder alternate slow and fast pitches to simulate bunting off-speed pitches.

Coaching Points

The bunter tries to adjust to balls out of the strike zone and balls that are moving a bit; most important, she works on "deadening" the ball and maintaining soft hands. This is especially hard to do off the machine because the machine tends to produce a lot of spin, which makes balls kick off the bat. Watch for all proper techniques discussed earlier, including proper timing of the turn, high hands, good bat angle, covering the plate, bent knees, and pinching the bat. Challenge bunters to bunt the ball within the cones. You can turn this into a competitive game for the entire team.

Purpose

To reinforce proper bunting mechanics for pitches at different locations in the strike zone; to gives athletes time to move correctly into proper position without worrying about contacting a moving pitch

Organization

Place a standard size tee and a ball at a base or home plate. The hitter holds a bat and stands in proper batting position. You can have a pitcher mock her throw, or the hitter can work on visualizing a pitcher throwing the ball.

Execution

Using varying tee heights (e.g., 10 balls high in the zone, 10 balls in the middle, 10 balls low), have the batter work on turning and simulating bunting the ball off the tee. She does not actually bunt the ball. Along with changing the height of the tee, you can move the tee up or back so the batter can work on bunting balls on the inside or outside of the plate. She should bunt balls to the right side, middle, and left side.

Variations

Call out locations on the field at which you want batters to place the bunt. As batters pivot and turn, they can alter the angle of the bat. Another variation is to have the bunter stand in her hitting stance with her eyes closed while a coach adjusts the tee and ball to different locations. As the coach calls out "pivot," the bunter opens her eyes and pivots quickly to the proper position. This adds an element of quick reaction. You could also add in the shadow bunting variation from the previous drill. Use a live pitcher to simulate throwing a pitch so the bunter can work on timing and moving to the ball on the tee location. Videotaping this drill allows players to see some of their improper mechanics and fix them before they progress to bunting a moving ball.

Coaching Points

Watch the bunter to make sure she can move to the pitch, especially the lower pitch. Make sure that the barrel of the bat is at eye level and that the bunter moves to the lower pitch with her legs. Keep an eye on the angle of the bat's barrel; it shouldn't drop and cause a pop-up bunt. Have your bunter work on visualizing the pitcher, the pitch coming toward her, laying the bunt down, and where the ball goes. Don't allow bunters simply to move the bat on low pitches. Watch for proper eye-to-bat-to-ball alignment. Educate players about the physics of a ball rebounding off a bat and how they can control the direction of the ball as it leaves the bat. Many teams don't have enough tees for every player on the team, so it might be best to run this drill along with a hitting rotational drill.

Purpose

To work on the mechanics of the sacrifice bunt, especially on having "soft hands" as players "catch" the ball with the bat; to teach contact points and good bat control

Organization

You'll need a bucket of balls, a home plate, a bat, and a helmet. You might set up a camera on a tripod to videotape the drill. This drill can be done in a cage or on the field. The coach positions about 10 feet (3 meters) in front of home plate, facing the hitter. A coach front tosses the ball. You might line players up and have them rotate through however many stations of coaches you have available. Or partner players up, and if they're good enough at it, they can front toss to each other.

Execution

The coach front tosses the ball; the player executes the bunt. The coach pitches the ball from a half-circle motion, not a full circle or windmill motion. As the coach's arm swings back, the bunter pivots into proper position to bunt the ball. The coach can vary the location and speed, depending on the skill level of the bunter. Each bunter should complete one bucket of balls; then switch bunters. If players are tossing to each other, they should switch roles when the bucket is empty. If you have several coaches on your staff and would rather they control the pace and quality of the drill, have them be the front tossers and rotate players through.

Variations

A fun variation to reinforce catching the ball on the bat is to have your bunters put their fielding glove on their top hand (the hand closer to the barrel of the bat) and hold the bat with that gloved hand. This might require players to put their glove on the opposite hand than the one they normally catch with. This variation should give players the feeling of softening the contact with the bat as they "catch" the ball rather than push it or slap it. Another variation is to add cones in a semicircle 10 to 12 feet (3 to 3.5 meters) in front of the bunter so she can work on keeping the ball inside the cones. Or you can put cones down on the 1B and 3B side of the field and have batters work on bunting to the right side and then the left side.

Coaching Points

Watch for timing of the rotation and proper "catching" of the ball on the bat technique. Encourage bunters to use bat angle to bunt to specific locations. Bunters should bunt only balls that are strikes, pulling the bat back on pitches outside the strike zone. Using the cone variation can give bunters immediate feedback on softening the bunt. Finally, when you have each bunter execute a full bucket, bunters should be required to rotate back to their hitting stance between each bunt attempt. This keeps the action gamelike.

Purpose

To work on bunting to very specific locations, such as a spot on the infield

Organization

This drill requires either a machine or a pitcher and a bucket of balls. Each bunter should have a helmet and a bat ready to go in the on-deck circle. A home plate is also needed. Draw sections in the dirt in front of home plate (or use cones to signify sections). In each section write a number representing a point value based on what the coach considers to be the perfect bunt. Remember that the machine balls tend to have more bounce, so you might want to make the sections larger if you use a machine.

Execution

Divide players into two teams. Team 1 starts on offense and team 2 on defense. The defensive team simply waits for the ball to stop and then picks it up and returns it to the feeder or bucket. The bunters on team 1 execute their bunts, attempting to get the most points based on the system already described. After every player has taken her turn, a scorekeeper should total up the points for each team and reward the winners.

Variation

Using a live pitcher makes this drill more gamelike. If each team has its own pitcher, bunters compete against the opposing pitcher. With this variation, you'll probably want to have a coach calling balls and strikes. If the pitcher walks a batter, her team loses a point.

Coaching Points

The focus of this drill is location, so before you begin it's a good idea to discuss why certain locations are better to bunt to than others, depending on the situation. In many situations, the ideal place to bunt the ball is in the area between the pitcher and either 1B or 3B. This drill helps players learn to place value on the "short game" (bunting). Players who don't hit for power but who are adept at bunting are recognized as crucial to the success of the team.

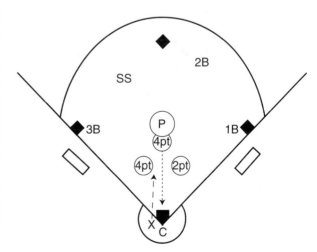

Purpose

To teach bunters to disguise the bunt and use all variations of the short game effectively, including the sacrifice, the slap bunt, the push bunt, the squeeze bunt, and the drag bunt

Organization

You need a home plate and a fastpitch softball machine set up on a regulation softball field, or in a cage. The bunter needs a bat and a helmet. Set up a screen in front of the machine and the ball feeder.

Execution

Place the team in groups of three or four. Each bunter steps in the box for one at-bat. Each group stays on offense for four or five rounds before rotating. Bunters execute a slap bunt, sacrifice, squeeze bunt, drag bunt, or push bunt. The defense calls out which type of bunt is being attempted as soon as they recognize it. If the bunter gives away clues by how she stands or holds the bat, this of course aids the defense. The bunter's job is to (1) give the defense no clues on what kind of bunt she will try and (2) execute the bunt successfully.

Variation

Have a coach call out the type of bunt to be executed before the ball is fed into the machine. This creates an element of pressure because players must respond quickly to the particular bunt. (In this variation, the defense obviously doesn't need to call out the type of bunt.)

Coaching Points

Your players should be well educated in the different types of bunts prior to this drill. By using the machine, you keep the timing of the pitches and the preparation consistent. Focus on players being deceptive with their bunts as well as on proper execution and timing. Keep an eye on the different hand or bat positions that bunters use for the slap bunt versus the drag bunt or sacrifice. Advanced bunters can get very good at tricking the defense by showing one kind of bunt and then laying down another.

Purpose

To work on several types of bunts in a realistic and gamelike situation; to improve on execution of the sacrifice bunt, slap bunt, push bunt, and squeeze bunt

Organization

You'll need a regulation fastpitch softball diamond, a fastpitch machine and balls, and a screen to protect the feeder. Divide the team into two groups. Your offensive team will all have helmets on and will be bunters and runners. Your defensive team will take infield positions and, if you have enough players, outfield positions as well. Have at least one offensive player with her helmet on near each base as well as an on-deck batter.

Execution

The defensive team captain or coach calls out the situation. Any situation is okay except for bases loaded or no runners at all. The offensive team takes bases according to the situation that has been called. The offensive team captain (who's coaching 3B) signals the offense on what type of bunt the batter will attempt. (If using a live pitcher, she should be throwing lots of strikes to keep the focus on execution.) The batter attempts the bunt, and the defense attempts to get the lead runner, if possible. If the offense executes the play and advances the runner, they score a point. If the defense gets the lead runner or keeps the runners from advancing with a pop-up or other out, they score a point. The next offensive batter steps in, and the process is repeated. Offensive team members should rotate until everyone on the team gets one at-bat. Switch teams and execute the drill the same way with the new bunting group. The game continues for a set number of rounds or until one team reaches a set number of points.

Variation

Put a coach in charge of signaling which bunts batters should attempt instead of using a player. This might result in a greater mix of bunts.

Coaching Points

Hitting is not an option in this drill, which forces players to play the game with only their short-game tools. Having players do the coaching gives them an appreciation for the value of the short game and the options that might work effectively. This drill is extremely helpful for hitters who struggle with signals and picking them up in pressure situations. Mentally, your athletes will learn to see how different types of bunting can be difficult for the defense to play. Remember to focus on advancing the runners and not on whether the offensive team scores or not. Players should learn that putting the runner on 1B might not always be the best scenario. Even on defense, your players will continue to become confident in the value of the short game and the proper execution of advancing runners.

GAME DAY SQUEEZE PLAY

Purpose

To help a bunter and a base runner work together on the timing of the squeeze bunt play; to give bunters experience in executing a squeeze under gamelike conditions

Organization

Split the team into two groups: offense and defense. Keep in mind that you want infielders in each group. The seven fielders can spread themselves in their true positions in the infield and then fill in the outfield as much as possible. You need either a pitching machine, balls, and a feeder or a live pitcher with someone feeding balls to her. The bunter needs her bat and helmet. There will be runners *only* at 3B and a bunter on deck. If available, a coach stands at 3B to give signals and to work with the runners to get an aggressive leadoff with the pitcher's release.

Execution

The hitter receives the signal from the coach. She gives the coach a return signal to show that she has read the signal. She then steps into the box and faces the pitcher (or machine). She waits for the pitcher to get into her windup and then squares late and executes the squeeze. As soon as the pitcher releases the ball, the runner breaks from 3B, without hesitation. Your defense can execute the play and attempt to get the runner out. If your defense is cheating too much, draw them a line to stay behind until the ball has been bunted.

Coaching Points

Review the key points of the squeeze bunt before you begin this drill. Getting the ball down in fair territory is the first priority. Location is the second priority. Have players discuss the best spots on the field in which to bunt to yield the most success in squeeze situations. Reiterate that the purpose of this drill is to work through all aspects of the squeeze bunt; encourage them to stop the drill as necessary to ask questions.

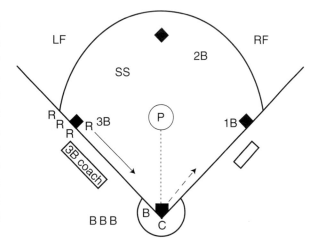

Purpose

To get many repetitions of the "sneaky bunt," also known as the drag bunt or bunting for a base hit; to practice squaring late to hide the bunt until the last possible moment

Organization

Place three or four batters in a row along a fence. Each batter should have a bat and a helmet. Place players far enough apart that they can safely square and bunt a thrown ball without interfering with each other. A single coach should have a bucket of balls and be standing about 30 feet (about 9 meters) or less from the hitters. If you have enough portable home plates, use one for each hitter along the fence. Otherwise use gloves or bucket lids.

Execution

The coach throws underhand (preferably) to the first bunter on the left, who does not square until the coach releases the ball. She attempts to put down a sneaky bunt. The coach then throws to the next batter, who also squares late to lay down a sneaky bunt. The coach continues to throw to each player down the row and then turns back to the first player on the left and begins again with the first player. The drill continues until the bucket of balls is gone.

Variations

Use Wiffle balls or light-weight softies at first so players are not afraid at such a close distance. Add more bunters to form a semicircle or circle around the coach. But remember that bunters need plenty of space between them so they don't foul balls off at each other.

Coaching Points

Timing is one of the most important principles with the sneaky, or drag, bunt. Make sure bunters don't rotate before the ball is released. Bunters may choke up more on the sneaky, or drag, bunt for greater control of the bat with the late rotation. Your bunters should bunt and take one step toward first base to simulate the actual drag bunt movement. Watch for bunters stepping onto the plate when they rotate late. Many batters panic and inadvertently move onto the plate.

Purpose

To put all of the bunts learned thus far together in a drill that includes live pitching and simulates a game as much as possible

Organization

All players are in game equipment and in their usual positions on the field. You need a live pitcher and someone to feed her balls. You also need a tee for the second player on deck. This tee can be placed down the line past the on-deck circle or off to the side near 3B with a screen in front to protect the player.

Execution

The live pitcher throws to a catcher who is giving the target for the pitcher. The bunter takes the signal from the coach and performs the bunt. She stands in there for three to five pitches, until the coach tells her to run out the last bunt and run through 1B (or else to turn and try for 2B, based on whatever happens with the play on the field). The runner at each bag plays out each bunt and tries to advance as far as she can. Let faster base runners lap slower ones. The catcher can jump out and field bunted balls.

Variations

If you have an advanced team, add the element of the fake bunt–steal play to this drill. This play entails having your bunters attempt to execute a bunt for a base hit but then miss the ball on purpose. The runner at 2B will take off with the release of the pitch, and what you're hoping for is a commitment by the third baseman to go after the bunt. You also hope she hesitates in getting back to the bag. If this hesitation occurs, and if the SS doesn't cover 3B, the player running to 3B will have a good chance of a successful steal. For this play to work, you need to have bunters who can sell the missed bunt and runners who are quick and aggressive enough to get in under a possible quick tag.

Coaching Points

Your bunters should be working on good timing and execution with the sacrifice bunt, the push bunt, the slap bunt, and the element of surprise on the sneaky bunt. In addition, you may instruct your pitcher to throw a bad pitch every once in a while to test the hitter on reading the pitch. Your runners should be working on good technique and reading the short-game executions. Runners should be aggressive but also use their heads to make smart decisions. It might be a good idea to videotape this session to give your players feedback on their mistakes. This drill might seem as if it moves very fast for some players, so the more you run it, the more comfortable they'll likely become. Any type of full situational defense that you can put your players into will prepare them for surprises that occur in games and help them make good, quick decisions.

Chapter 8

Slap Hitting

Heather Tarr *University of Washington Head Coach*

Slap hitting has proven to be a necessary asset to any offense in the game of fastpitch softball. It is said that "speed never slumps." While this is true, speed isn't everything. At the higher levels of softball, a player with good speed but poor slapping mechanics will inevitably slump. The mechanics and skills of the left-handed slap need to be taught and developed correctly and efficiently so players can execute this hit in games.

Execute most of the drills in this chapter daily with your players to develop proper muscle memory and discipline. A left-handed slapper can have many tools in her toolbox. A slapper with many tools might at times need your direction to make the best pre-at-bat decision, but it's important to emphasize to young players how to read a defense and recognize on their own which tool to use in particular situations. An effective slapper knows how to execute the bunt to keep the defense honest. At the higher levels of softball, slappers should know how to hit away; at lower levels, this is not absolutely necessary.

When executing the slap, the player must understand what she is trying to do with the ball. The idea behind the skill is to hit the ball to a place on the infield that's farthest from the place where the out needs to be made. For example, with nobody on base, the out needs to be made at first base, so the slapper will usually attempt to get the ball to the shortstop's backhand side. When there's a runner at second base, the slapper might try to hit for the situation and move the runner over from second to third by hitting the ball to the second baseman. A question here is does the hitter want to drive the ball in the hole (with a line drive) or bounce the ball? A good slapper can do either. She decides before the pitch (or even before her at-bat) which type of slap she'll attempt. A good slapper tries to never hit a one bouncer to the defense. The base hit usually is a line drive through the defense, a two bouncer, or a high chopper. Bouncing the ball doesn't allow the slapper enough time to beat out the ball to first . If the slapper can make the ball bounce twice to the shortstop, there's usually enough time to beat the throw to first. A slapper should never simply hit a "ground out" and attempt to beat the throw. She'll always want to bounce the ball or hit a line drive. The playing surface and particular pitcher usually determine if a bounce or line drive is a better choice.

Several basic drills are covered in this chapter. All great slappers maintain a disciplined approach, regardless of the situation. Proper muscle memory must be developed for this to occur. The slapping mechanics and drills described in this chapter will help your players succeed at all levels of the game.

Purpose

To understand proper hand path and contact points and body positioning for the slapper

Organization

You'll need a tee, balls, and either a catch net or an open area in which to hit balls.

Execution

Have the batter arrive at her crossover position of the slap (back foot crossed over the front). She should stay in that position and make sure her hands are in a proper "launch position" to throw the bat to the ball. To simulate an outside pitch, begin by working on the outside contact point (usually the easiest for the slapper to handle if she has good mechanics, and the toughest if her mechanics are poor). Make sure she goes through the proper passage to arrive at the slapping position. She'll attempt either to line drive the ball or bounce it by choosing the part of the ball she hits (top half or middle). To simulate a middle pitch, move the tee to the middle of the plate and line drive or bounce the ball to the desired spot on the field. To simulate an inside pitch, move the tee to the inside part of the plate and do the same. A slapper with good mechanics will have the toughest time taking the inside pitch up the middle or to the SS because her hands have to work inside the ball in an extreme fashion to get the angle she wants.

Variation

Change the plane of the tee as well as the contact point.

Coaching Points

The slapper remains in her slapping position through contact. Her head should remain steady, with eyes on the contact point throughout the swing. The slapper isolates her bottom half to maximize understanding and muscle memory of the hand path to the contact points (inside, middle, outside). She should reset her feet every two to three swings so that she pays attention to where she is in relation to the ball or contact point. Her body should remain stationary throughout the swing with her weight staying on the back leg through the swing.

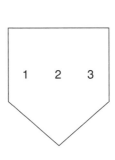

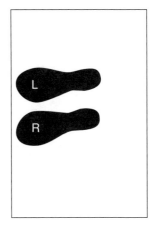

93   FOUR CORNERS OFF THE TEE

Purpose
To help players understand proper hand path, contact points, and body positioning for the slapper

Organization
You'll need a tee, balls, and either a catch net or an open area in which to hit balls.

Execution
The batter should arrive at her crossover position of the slap (back foot crossed over the front). She'll work on the quadrants of the strike zone. Have her hit the ball to the SS backhand side with balls located at each of the corners of the strike zone: down and away, up and away, up and in, and down and in.

Variation
Have the slapper do this drill by going through her passage.

Coaching Points
Communicate regularly with the slapper to test her knowledge of angles and how to bounce or line drive the ball from each contact point. Make sure the mechanics of the passage stay sound. Note that a slapper doesn't always have to hit the ball to the 5 to 6 hole. She can work on hitting the ball where it's pitched, or work on hitting behind the runner for each of the corners of the zone.

94 HORSE

Purpose
To work on understanding proper hand path, contact points, and body positioning for the slapper

Organization
You'll need a tee, balls, and either a catch net or an open area in which to hit balls. Two players (or a player and a coach) participate in this drill. The slapper should have a visual idea of where the infield defense would be in relation to the catch net or batting cage.

Execution
The batter arrives at her crossover position of the slap (back foot crossed over the front). Have the slapper that goes first call her shot (e.g., "I'm going to bounce the ball to the SS" or "I'm going to line drive this ball to the SS." She has all kinds of options here.) Players must use their knowledge of the contact points and how to create angles on the ball with the bat. If the slapper that calls her shot first misses her "call," the next slapper comes up to bat and makes her call. If she makes her shot (if her slap goes where she called it), the next batter must make the exact same "shot" or else earn an H. The next time she misses a shot the other player has made, she receives an O. Subsequent missed plays result in an R, an S, and finally an E, at which point she is eliminated.

Variation
Have the slapper do this drill by going through her passage.

Coaching Points
Monitor players' knowledge of angles and how to bounce or line drive the ball to their called spots. When the slapper is in her slapping position, make sure her hands are in a proper "launch" position to throw the bat to the ball. The slapper will be isolating her bottom half (her legs) to maximize understanding and muscle memory of the hand path to the contact points (inside, middle, outside).

Purpose

To promote proper understanding of hand path and body positioning for the slapper

Organization

You'll need a pitching screen, balls, and a home plate. The batter stands at the plate; the pitcher (coach) stands behind the screen.

Execution

The batter assumes her crossover position of the slap (back foot crossed over the front). The pitcher pitches the ball with a soft toss from behind the screen. The slapper stays in her slapping position to isolate her bottom half and uses her hands to get to the proper part of the ball. Have the slapper hit the ball where you pitch it to the called point on the field. You can have batters work on hitting the ball to any spot on the field by bouncing the ball or line driving it. The slapper will remain in slapping position through contact.

Variation

Change the distance from where you're tossing so that the slapper must adjust her timing without changing her posture.

Coaching Points

Her head should remain steady with her eyes on the contact point through the swing. She should reset her feet every two to three swings so that she pays attention to where she is in relation to the ball or contact point. Her body should remain stationary with her weight on her back leg throughout the swing. Make sure she swings at strikes! Finally, don't allow her to swing without a purpose. Give her a purpose until she understands how to do this on her own.

Purpose
To train understanding of proper timing and footwork for the slapper

Organization
You'll need a pitching screen, balls, and a home plate. The batter stands at the plate; the pitcher (coach) stands behind the screen.

Execution
The batter assumes the crossover position of the slap (back foot crossed over the front). The coach tells the slapper what to do with the ball—either line drive it or bounce it. The coach tosses the ball with a soft toss from behind the screen. The slapper starts toward the pitcher when she sees the ball leave the tosser's hand. The slapper should be sure to use proper foot placement as she moves through the batter's box. Watch for athletes who step onto home plate or out of the batter's box.

Variation
Change the distance of the tossing point so the slapper must adjust her timing without changing her body posture. The slapper should think, *Throw hands to the ball when I see it.*

Coaching Points
Make sure the slapper stays disciplined with her passage. Watch her drop step to make sure it's keeping her in line (not pulling off the ball). Make sure the slapper continues toward the pitcher to ensure she's focusing on staying on the ball and throwing the bat to the ball. She should track the ball to the contact point. Encourage the slapper to begin to make her own decision on whether to bounce the ball or hit a line drive. Don't let her just ground out.

Purpose

To develop proper muscle memory for the timing and execution of specific slaps

Organization

You'll need a pitching screen, balls, and a home plate. The batter stands at the plate; the tosser (coach) stands behind the screen.

Execution

This is a competition among several players. The tosser stands behind the screen and pitches the ball with a soft toss. She directs the slapper where to hit the ball on the field. Have the slapper hit the ball to the called point on the field. When the slapper doesn't execute the called skill, she is out until the next round begins. The player who remains when all other players have been eliminated is the winner.

Coaching Points

This drill can be done with a machine. Continue to monitor body positioning and make sure players swing at strikes.

Purpose

To work on rhythm and timing of the slap

Organization

You need a tennis ball, a bat, and a tosser.

Execution

The slapper assumes her stance. The slapper goes through a dry run of her passage so the tosser can judge the distance of the slapper's passage. The tosser should understand where she needs to bounce the tennis ball so that it arrives at the general area of the strike zone. The tosser bounces the ball so that it crosses the strike zone. The slapper judges when she needs to start her slap to hit the ball to the desired location on the field, and she hits to that location.

Variations

Have the tosser mix in a ball that's out of the strike zone to see if the slapper takes the pitch. Work on all three contact points: inside, middle, and outside.

Coaching Points

Make sure the slapper doesn't sacrifice mechanics; watch her timing and rhythm. The emphasis of this drill is to understand where to make contact with different locations of the bounced ball. Make sure the slapper follows through with her passage toward the pitcher and keeps her head on the ball through contact.

Purpose
To work on pitch recognition for the slap; to understand how to work the hands to the high pitch and the low pitch

Organization
You'll need a pitching screen, a home plate, balls, and a bat. The batter stands at the plate; the pitcher stands behind the screen in front of the batter.

Execution
The tosser pitches the ball to the slapper. The ball should be directed either at the top of the strike zone or the bottom of the strike zone. The slapper goes through her passage to the ball. For every high pitch, she hits a line drive. For every low pitch, she bounces the ball.

Variations
Have the tosser pitch from different positions so the slapper must adjust her timing. Work on all three contact points: inside, middle, and outside.

Coaching Points
Make sure the slapper doesn't sacrifice mechanics; watch her timing and rhythm. Emphasize hitting either a line drive or bouncing the ball; don't just let her "ground out." Make sure the slapper follows through with her passage toward the pitcher and keeps her head on the ball through contact.

Purpose

To work on timing and rhythm of the passage; to promote understanding of where the hands need to be for the slap at contact

Organization

You'll need a pitching screen, a home plate, balls, and a bat. The batter stands at the plate; the pitcher stands behind the screen in front of the batter. You can run this drill off a live pitcher, a machine, or a batting tee.

Execution

The tosser pitches the ball to the slapper. The batter goes through her passage at full speed and stops the bat at contact. Make sure she continues to move through the slap; she should *not* stop her body at contact. Only her hands stop at contact. The tosser should pitch the ball inside and out, which requires the batter to adjust on the fly to different pitch locations.

Variation

Have the tosser move back and forth so the slapper must adjust her timing.

Coaching Points

Make sure the slapper understands when she needs to start her slapping passage. She should follow through with her passage toward the pitcher and keep her head on the ball through contact. She should focus on understanding timing. Have her adjust when she starts her hands to the ball to emphasize letting the ball get deep into the hitting zone. See how deep she can let the ball travel and still keep it in fair territory.

Purpose

To work on body positioning, direction, and keeping the head and eyes stationary throughout the slap

Organization

All you need is a full-length mirror and a bat or a stick.

Execution

The slapper gets in her stance. She's facing the mirror as if the mirror is the pitcher. The batter goes through her slap while watching herself in the mirror. She should first go through her passage and visualize taking a pitch. She should then go through her passage and visualize slapping a ball to a specific location with a specific pitch in mind. Have her exhaust all types of slaps with all types of pitch locations (use the four corners of the strike zone as a reference).

Variations

Use a Wiffle ball off a tee going into the mirror. Make sure the mirror is thick enough to take a hit with the Wiffle ball. Have the hitter watch herself actually slapping a ball. Another variation is to have the hitter change the angle at which she's looking at herself. Have her turn sideways and do the same drills from a different (perpendicular) perspective.

Coaching Points

Make sure the slapper doesn't start too close to the mirror. Have her note where her hands are on the crossover. She should remain in a good launch position with her shoulder on the ball.

Position-Specific Drills

Chapter 9

Infielder

Kim Sowder Long Beach State Head Coach

Infielders are often called the best athletes on the field. To be a great infielder you must have athletic ability, quickness, a great work ethic, and a constant drive to become better. Because infielders are located in the middle of the field, they're in position to communicate with everyone on the field, constantly supporting the pitcher and always informing the outfield of the number of outs, the type of hitter, and what pitches are being thrown. Defense is a key component to all championship teams, and the infield plays a big part of the defense. The defense not only keeps the other team from scoring but also plays an important role in creating momentum for its own team's offense. Many teams' offenses feed off their team's defense. The fewer mistakes made equates to less time on defense and more time on offense. Nothing fires up an offense more than an infielder making a spectacular play to take away a run and end an inning.

Infielders must be ready to move in all directions and field balls at a variety of speeds. Infielders should view defense as an *action* rather than a reaction. Infielders need to be aggressive and ready to make a play on the ball instead of reacting to what the ball does. Four of the most important abilities all infielders must have and constantly work to improve on are reading the ball off the bat, moving their feet quickly, dominating the ball with the glove, and throwing with a quick release. Good infield drills will help with one or more of these areas of importance.

Infielders have many different responsibilities when they step onto the field, so they must be both physically and mentally prepared. The first thing all infielders should do when standing at their position is to be aware of the situation. They should know the score, the number of outs, how many runners are on base, the speed of the runners, the type of hitter at bat, and the possible scenarios that can occur depending on how and where the batter hits the ball. It's also important to know what your coach wants you to do in certain situations. All infielders must know all of these things before the pitcher steps onto the mound. If they have thought about all the possible situations prior to the pitch, there's much less chance for any hesitation or error once the ball is in play.

The next skill that an infielder must develop (or continue to develop) is reading the ball off the bat. Because of ongoing advancements in the technology of bats and balls, the speed of the ball off the bat is now faster than ever. This being the case, infielders must continue to become quicker at reading the ball off the bat. This can be done by focusing on where the pitch is in relation to the hitter's bat. Infielders should try to read if the hitter is late or early and the type of swing the hitter has. Does the hitter have a big swing that goes around the pitch? Or does the hitter stay inside the ball? Infielders should try to read as soon as possible whether the ball is going to be hit to the right or left. Focus on this in practice. Another great time to work on this is during shag time for batting practice. Infielders should try to read every hit as early as possible.

The drills in this chapter help players to improve on the basic fundamentals they need to play the infield. These drills are for all infielders and work on a variety of skills required of these players. The drills focus on reading the ball off the bat, pre-pitch routines, first step and crossover footwork, angles to the ball, dominating the ball with the glove, quick feet, quick release, accuracy, flips, strength, conditioning, and, most important, concentration.

The essential thing to remember when running these drills is to challenge your players. Your players should be committed to the drill and try to make every play. Working the fundamentals of the game and becoming stronger, quicker, more consistent, and more confident with them every day is of such importance. If your infielders make only 90 percent of their plays in practice, they're going to make only 90 percent of their plays in games as well. If they make 99 percent of their plays in practice, they're going to make 99 percent of their plays in the game. This includes every play they make during practice, whether it's warming up their arms, doing individual drills, or participating in team drills. The difference between a good infielder and a great infielder is the level of concentration in practice day in and day out.

Purpose

To work on an infielder's quickness and ability to stay low to the ground when fielding ground balls

Organization

Position two players facing each other about five feet (1.5 meters) apart. Player A, the tosser, starts with two balls in her hand and kneeling down on one knee. Player B, the fielder, starts in a ready position without a glove.

Execution

Player A rolls the ball about five feet to the left of where the fielder is standing. The fielder, in a low ready position, shuffles to the left and fields the ball out in front with two hands. She quickly tosses the ball back underhand to the tosser. Once the ball is in the air back to the tosser, the tosser rolls the other ball five feet to the right of the fielder, and the fielder shuffles quickly to the right to field it. This drill continues back and forth for 30 seconds, when the coach blows the whistle. The fielder should keep her knees bent for the entire drill without any hunch in her back.

Variations

Use this drill at any skill level and for any period of time. Consider keeping the time at 30 seconds or less so fielders can work at 100 percent speed for the entire drill. Coaches for younger players might shorten the time to 15 seconds.

Coaching Points

The focus of the drill is on staying low by bending the knees rather than the back. Make sure the fielder doesn't stand to toss the ball. Make sure the tosser is challenging the fielder by making the fielder move as fast as she can.

Purpose

To work on an infielder's ability to dominate the ball with the glove when fielding short hops

Organization

Position two fielders about 10 feet (3 meters) apart facing each other. One player will be the thrower; the other will field short hops. The fielder should be in ready position.

Execution

The tosser throws the ball so that it lands anywhere from 1 to 3 feet (.3 to 1 meter) in front of the fielder. The fielder should be in a low ready position with her glove close to the ground. As the ball is in flight, the fielder moves to the ball, catching it immediately after it touches the ground. The fielder should be aggressive to the ball, focusing on catching it in the pocket of her glove. Tell your infielders to "dominate the ball."

The throwing hand should be next to the glove, ready to cover and retrieve the ball quickly. The player can either toss the ball to the side or toss it back to her partner.

Variations

The thrower can throw balls directly in front of the fielder, to the left of the fielder, or to the right of the fielder. The fielder moves her feet in the direction of the throw, trying to remain in front of the ball.

Coaching Points

Make sure fielders are staying on the balls of their feet and not on their heels. If a fielder gets on her heels, she'll have a hard time moving to the ball, and her head will be too high to see the ball into her glove.

Purpose

To work on proper technique for fielding ground balls on the run

Organization

Start with all infielders in a single line. A coach begins with a bucket of softie balls or tennis balls.

Execution

The coach should bounce a ball toward the first player in line. The player begins to run and continues to run through the ball as she fields. Players need to learn to get low and field from the ground up as they run toward the coach. Once the player fields the ball she continues to run toward the coach and drops the ball into the bucket.

Variations

This drill can be done with tennis balls and bare handed, or the coach can bounce softie balls and players use their gloves. As a variation, put players at their actual infield positions and have them throw home or to 1B while on the run.

Coaching Points

Make sure players keep their palms up toward the sky as they field. They should always approach the ball with the fielding hand or glove below the ball (called "fielding from the ground up"). Many players swing or swat at the ball, which should be avoided because it makes for limited success. Tennis balls and bare-hand fielding make this a very safe drill; players won't fear being hit by the ball on a bad bounce.

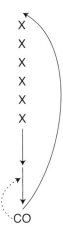

Purpose
To give first basemen work on receiving balls at 1B; to train staying on the bag unless they must leave the bag to make a catch

Organization
You'll need one coach with a bat and a bucket of balls to stand at the SS position. The first baseman stands at the 1B bag with glove in position to receive a ball from the SS (coach).

Execution
The coach at SS hits a line drive to the first baseman. The first baseman stands at 1B just as she would if she were receiving a throw from the SS. The first baseman reads the hit and stretches to where the ball is thrown or comes off the bag as necessary. The coach hits one ball after another until all balls have been used. Because the balls are being hit, the first baseman gets a good variety of balls to catch. The object is to catch everything and not let any balls get by.

Variations
Move the hitter around to different areas on the infield. Include a catcher at home plate, and have the first baseman work on catching the ball at 1B and making the throw to the plate.

Coaching Points
Make sure that your first baseman is not stretching for the ball too early. She should read the hit and then stretch to the ball. If your first baseman has to leave the bag to make the catch, be sure to have them make a fake tag. Emphasize how important it is that she comes off the bag if necessary so that the runner doesn't end up at 2B. This drill is fun for first basemen because it's challenging and different from someone just standing and throwing balls at them.

Purpose

To work on fielding ground balls, getting throws off quickly, conditioning, and concentration

Organization

Place two hitters about 70 feet (21.3 meters) apart on the infield. Each hitter will need a player to catch for her and to toss her balls. Position a fielding player with a glove between the two hitters.

Execution

Hitter 1 hits a ground ball to the fielder, who fields the ball quickly and throws to catcher 1. The fielder then quickly turns around and fields another ball hit by hitter 2 and throws to catcher 2. This process continues back and forth until the fielder fields a set number of ground balls. Note that each hitter should begin to hit her ground ball as soon as the fielder has released the ball to the opposite side.

Variation

Make this drill as tough as you want. It is recommended that each fielder field anywhere from 20 to 30 ground balls. If you think a fielder is taking her time getting rid of the ball and working at half-speed, keep her in the box longer. You can make this drill a competition by hitting all players the same number of balls and counting how many they field and throw cleanly.

Coaching Points

Players are working on reaction to the ball and getting rid of the ball quickly, as if for a close play. The drill is harder than it sounds. Players will tire and must concentrate more than ever by the end of the drill. You must keep the drill moving to make it work, so have plenty of spare balls next to your catchers in case of a bad throw or hit. You can run this drill at the beginning of practice to get your players' minds and bodies warmed up. Have players not involved in the "hot box" watch and give encouragement from the sidelines.

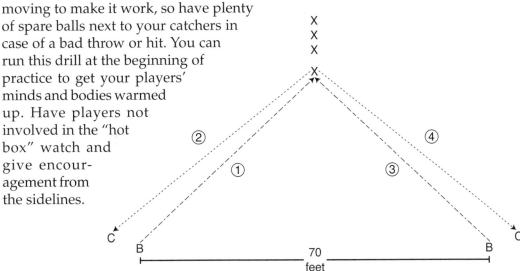

Purpose

To work on the approach to each pitch and being in a position to react quickly in either direction

Organization

A coach has a bucket of balls; a player is at her position with her glove. The coach sets up between the fielder and home plate about 20 feet (6 meters) from the fielder. You can work this drill for all infield positions.

Execution

The coach, either on one knee or standing up, uses a slingshot motion to roll the ball to the fielder. As the coach moves his or her arm in backward motion, the fielder walks into the ready position with two steps. The fielder then continues to the ball, taking the proper angle to the ball and fielding it by going through the ball; she then sets up for her throw. The fielder should not stop her feet until she's into throwing position.

Coaching Points

Players create a rhythm by taking a step forward with each foot. Before the ball is released, the fielder should be in a relaxed position on the balls of her feet, ready to react. Make sure she's not still moving forward as the ball is released. Players should be loose and not too low to the ground. If they're too low, they'll have to stand up to move, which makes them slower to the ball. As the ball is released, the fielder reads the direction of the ball, pivots her foot (left if the ball is to the left, right if the ball is to the right), and crosses over with the opposite foot to move in the direction of the ball. The general rule is the closer you are to the plate, the lower your ready position. In almost all cases infielders will need to move before they field a ball. If your fielders are too low to start with, they'll lose time rising up to move.

Purpose

To help fielders read the ball off the bat and move their feet for different types of throws

Organization

You'll need a hitter at home plate and a tosser nearby with a bucket of balls. All infielders are at their positions with their gloves.

Execution

Begin the drill by designating one player to cover the field and receive the first five ground balls. All other infielders should cover a base to receive a throw from the designated fielder. The hitter (or coach) at home hits balls being tossed up from the tosser next to the plate. The first ball is hit gamelike off the bat for the fielder to read and field. A total of five balls will be hit to each fielder during her turn. The first ball should be thrown to 1B, the second ball should be thrown to 2B, the third to 3B, the fourth back to 2B, and the fifth back to 1B. After the first fielder receives her five grounders, the next fielder takes her turn, and the remaining fielders cover a base to receive throws. Each gets an opportunity to field five gamelike ground balls from the hitter or coach hitting side-toss fungos.

Variations

This drill can be done with a coach just hitting a ground ball and not from a side toss. The purpose of the side toss is to create a gamelike reaction of the ball off the bat. The first time you run this drill, you can roll rather than hit balls to the fielders so they can focus on their footwork and throws.

Coaching Points

This drill is gamelike for infielders, giving them a chance to read where a pitch is going and how a hitter reacts. Players need to be able to move their feet after fielding the ball to line up their throws to the bases. Each infielder should be able to switch directions and make throws after fielding a variety of types of ground balls.

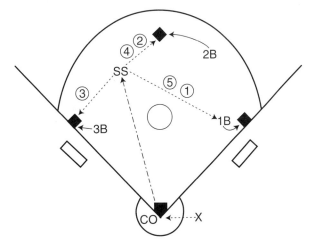

Purpose

To work on eye–hand coordination, staying low to the ground on grounders, and good footwork

Organization

A coach stands in the center of the field or on the pitcher's mound with a bucket of tennis balls or softies. Place eight cones in a circle around the coach about 15 feet (4.5 meters) away. This creates a 30-foot diameter circle around the coach with eight evenly spaced cones. Infielders take a position at each cone. There should be at least one open cone. Infielders should be either bare handed (if using tennis balls) or using a paddle or glove (if using softie balls).

Execution

The coach in the center of the circle designates which direction players will be moving (either to the forehand or backhand side). The coach rolls the first ball to the open cone next to the first player. That player works on her crossover step and fields the ball in the designated forehand or backhand position in front of the open cone. She then jogs to the center of the circle and drops the ball into the bucket. The coach immediately rolls the next ball to the cone that the first player vacated, and the second player pivots and cross-steps to field that ball; she'll then jog to the bucket, drop in the ball, and return to the cone from which she fielded. The process continues around the circle with the coach always rolling to the open cone and the next player aggressively moving to field the ball with proper technique in front of the open cone. Once all players have gone, switch directions and roll to the open cone with players moving in the opposite direction.

Variations

Coaches use this circle drill to get their players a number or reps quickly for all types of fielding skills. Tennis balls or softies can be bounced toward the open cone, and players can work on moving laterally and planting their feet aggressively to field the short hop. Coaches also use this drill to work on getting in front of balls to the forehand and backhand side. These variations are at the coach's discretion and will depend on how the balls are rolled or bounced to the open cone.

Coaching Points

This drill is helpful for players who need work on fielding balls to their backhand. For the fielder to be successful, she must keep her eye on the ball the entire play and stay very low to the ground. These are two key skills needed for the backhand. Because the balls are much smaller and no glove is used, players must focus on seeing the tennis balls all the way into their hands. Footwork is one of the most important skills required of good infielders, and this drill works a lot of reps at lateral footwork in both directions. Stress good technique.

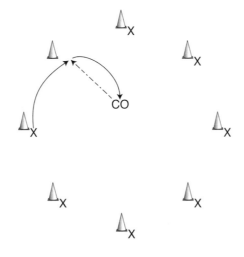

Purpose

To work footwork and proper technique on different types of throws needed in the infield

Organization

You'll need five or more players, a set of throw or portable bases, and a ball. This drill can be done outside on the dirt or inside on a gym or artificial floor. Place the bases about 15 feet (4.5 meters) apart to form a square. Put at least one player at every base and the extra player with the ball at one of the four bases. Each stage of this drill progressively increases the distance between the bases, eventually reaching a full 60 feet (18.2 meters).

Execution

For the first round, players work on the forehand toss. The player with the ball rolls the ball to the player at the next base in clockwise direction. The next player steps in to field the ball with proper technique and then turns and tosses a forehand toss to the next player in the clockwise position. Meanwhile, the first player is sprinting to the same base that she just rolled the ball toward. Other players similarly sprint to the base that they throw to immediately after releasing the ball. The player who receives the forehand toss catches the ball and places a tag at the base and then immediately rolls the ball to the next player, and the process is repeated. Players always sprint and follow their roll or toss. After players have gone all the way around the bases and end up at the base at which they started, switch directions and work on the backhand side. Once players again return to their original base, move the bases out to about 30 feet (9.1 meters) apart. The drill goes back to the forehand direction, and players work on a drop-knee throw to the forehand side. After a complete rotation and players are back at their original bases, switch direction again to work on the backhand side. Players always sprint and follow their throws or rolls. Move the bases out to 50 feet (15.2 meters) and then out to a full 60 feet (18.2 meters), each time running the drill as described. Players work on their footwork for full throws around the bases in both directions.

Variations

Challenge the group by observing how many throws they can get in a set amount of time. Or observe how many bases or good throws the team can make without a bad or errant throw. To raise the difficulty and get increased technique focus, run this drill with players bouncing short hops to each other instead of rolling the ball.

Coaching Points

Work this drill in both directions. Make sure that players are placing proper tags down to the base after receiving each throw. Stress proper fielding technique. Good throws allow a player at the base to keep her feet set and not have to reach for the ball.

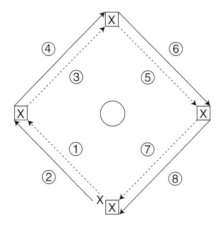

111   DOUBLE T

Purpose
To work on lateral quickness and up-and-back change of direction

Organization
Each player needs a glove. You'll also need two to four cones and a bucket of balls. A coach tosses the balls. Position the coach at home with the bucket of balls. Place a cone 15 feet (4.5 meters) on either side of the pitching rubber. If you have additional cones, place one next to the pitching rubber on either side. Divide infielders into two groups and place half of them at the cone on the left side of the infield and the other half at the cone on the right side of the field.

Execution
A single player at each cone goes first. The coach rolls the first ball toward the pitching rubber for the player on the left side of the field to pivot and field. The coach then immediately rolls a second ball toward the right side of the pitching rubber for the player at the right-side cone to field. Each player fields the ball and tosses it into the bucket on the pitching rubber or rolls it back toward the coach; she then gets into ready position at the point where she just fielded the ball. The coach then rolls a ball to the outside of the cone on the left side of the infield for the same player, who rotates and moves laterally back in the opposite direction. The coach then immediately rolls a ball to the outside of the cone on the right side of the field for the original player on the right to move laterally and field outside the cone. Players again either toss the ball into a bucket placed near the cone or roll it back toward the coach at home. Players get into their field positions at their new location near the cone. The coach then tosses a short pop fly in front of the player on the left side of the field so that she must spring forward to make the catch. Immediately afterward, the coach tosses a similar short pop fly in front of the player on the right side of the field to catch on the run. Both players toss the balls back to the coach's vicinity and return to the field position at which they caught the pop fly. Now the coach tosses a ball back over the shoulder of the player on the left side and then the same for the player on the right side. This completes the T on each side of the field. Each player makes a play in the four different directions. After a player completes the T on the left side, she rotates to the end of the line on the right side, and vice versa.

Variations
This drill can be done with bare hands and tennis balls—or with bare hands and real balls or full-size softies.

Coaching Points

This drill provides good practice for improving each infielder's ability to move in many different directions quickly. Watch for each player's first step in each direction. Players should not be using a false step or a negative step prior to stepping in the direction of the ball. On the lateral movement, players should use a pivot and crossover step to increase their range. Empty buckets can be placed nearby for players to toss into; make sure they're not tossing balls into the area in which they'll be running. As always, stress safety. If the pitcher's mound area is not level or is unsafe, set the drill up at another location on the field. This drill can be done with all fly balls. The lateral balls tossed can be line drives that players must sprint to.

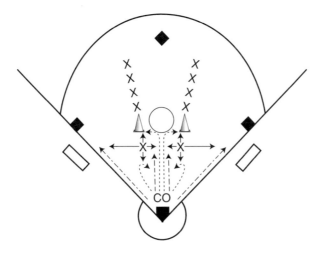

Chapter 10

Outfielder

Margie Wright   *Fresno State University Head Coach*

The outfield is one of the most overlooked areas in the game. Coaches need to always remember that players will perform in games similar to how they perform in practice. Coaches can only expect players to execute what coaches train them to do in practice. This means that coaches need to work with outfielders in practice and not just assume they'll perform in a game when they put them out there. There are many aspects to playing the outfield that players need to master to be successful, including great confidence in their fielding skills, ability to cover large areas with efficiency and speed, ability to make strong accurate throws under extreme pressure, and communication with all of the fielders on the field. Think about how many games are won or lost based on a single play or throw from the outfield late in the game. Great outfielders take tremendous pride in their role on their team and in the game of softball.

Former Fresno State University All-American and NCAA Champion Laura Berg is one of the greatest outfielders ever to play the game. To date, she is the only player to play centerfield for the USA Olympic team, winning gold medals in 1996, 2000, and 2004. She offers her thoughts on playing the grass:

> Outfielders are the last line of defense. When an infielder makes an error, 99 percent of the time it results in one extra base for the runner. But when an outfielder makes an error, the consequence is two or more bases, or even a gold medal or a championship. For example, in the 2000 Olympic gold medal game, the left fielder for Japan made a huge error: She back pedaled for a fly ball and dropped the ball as she fell to the ground. If she had turned and run to get to the ball, she would have caught it. Because of the mistake, Team USA won the gold medal. A successful outfielder needs to have the mentality that she is not going to let anything drop and should take it personally when a ball drops in the outfield. When a ball is hit in the air, she needs to find a way to catch the ball, whether she is diving for it, going through a fence, or going over a fence. As an outfielder, I want my pitcher to have the peace of mind that if a ball gets hit to the

grass, I will catch it. There's nothing like making that diving catch or throwing out a runner trying to advance an extra base. Some young ball players think outfield is boring—it's anything but boring! There is so much for an outfielder to do, and she has so much responsibility to her teammates. An outfielder has to communicate to other fielders, back up other fielders, and know where to throw the ball at all times. The outfield is where they put the *real* athletes—outfielders rule!

The outfielder needs to take pride in playing her position. There's a lot more to it than just catching fly balls and cutting off line drives. The drills presented in this chapter will help your outfielders hone the skills they need to be the best they can be at their positions.

Purpose

To improve conditioning and to work on catching the ball out in front on the glove and nonglove side

Organization

A coach with a bucket of balls faces a line of outfielders on the left-field sideline.

Execution

The first fielder steps up to the sideline. She begins running to catch a coach-tossed fly ball in left field. She makes the catch and throws the ball back to the coach (or to a player standing next to the coach). She then runs to centerfield to catch another tossed fly ball; again, she makes the catch and throws the ball in. She then proceeds to right field and repeats the process. After throwing the ball in, she jogs around the outfield, returns to the left-field line, and takes her place at the end of the line of players. The next player then steps up and performs the drill. After several repetitions for each player from the left-field line, the outfielders move to the right-field line to run the same drill.

Variations

This drill can be done with ground balls or without a throw in from the fielder. It can also be done in a smaller area or even in a gym.

Coaching Points

Watch for proper mechanics on the catch and throw. Outfielders should sprint to get ahead of the ball and watch it into their glove.

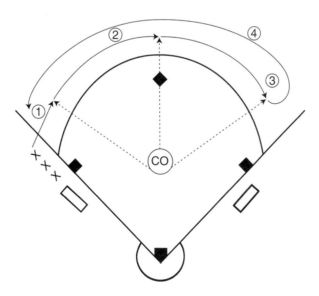

Purpose
To help players improve at fielding line drives on the run

Organization
You'll need two coaches (or tossers), two buckets of balls, two empty buckets, and two lines of players.

Execution
A coach tosses a line drive to the first player in line. The player sprints to catch the ball, makes the play, and continues running to the other line, where she puts the ball into the bucket and takes her place at the end of the line.

Variations
Position the lines of players on the other side of the tossers so they can catch balls on both the nonglove and glove side. Add throws from the fielder to the coach (or a player standing next to the coach). This can be done indoors or outdoors.

Coaching Points
Make sure outfielders are sprinting to the ball and not "timing" their catches. Each outfielder should catch the ball out in front of her body and watch the ball into her glove.

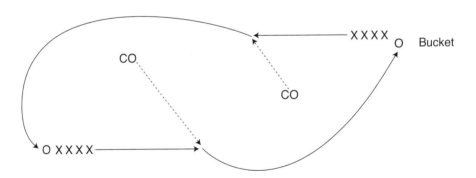

Purpose

To learn to use the drop step properly and practice changing direction while keeping eyes on the ball

Organization

A coach is behind 2B with a bucket of balls; a line of players is behind the coach. One player steps out and faces the coach.

Execution

Facing the player, the coach holds up a ball and points it to either the left or right. The player drop steps in that direction. The coach then holds the ball on the other side so that the player changes direction using a drop step. The coach changes direction one more time; the player drop steps and changes direction. The coach then throws a fly ball in that direction for the player to catch; the player makes the catch and then gets into position to throw back to the next player in line by the coach. She then takes her place at the end of the line, and the next player steps out.

Variations

This drill can be done in a small space or a gym. You can have players change direction as many times as you like. You could also do a blind drop step on a ball that's thrown farther away from the fielder on the last change of direction. (A blind drop step is turning your back to the ball and finding it after it has been thrown.)

Coaching Points

The goal is to execute a proper drop step and hustle to get behind the ball so it can be caught as a routine fly ball. Getting into position to make a good throw is key. Players also need to keep their eyes on the ball.

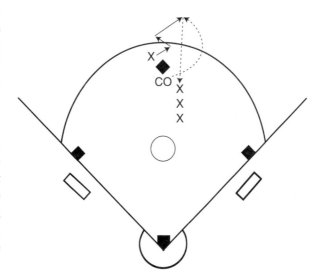

Purpose

To work on conditioning in position using proper technique and mechanics

Organization

A line of fielders stands behind a coach who is near 2B with a bucket of balls. Three players are needed in the field: one playing 2B, one at SS, and one near the coach to field throws. All other fielders are in the line facing the coach.

Execution

A player steps out of line to face the coach. The coach says, "Go!" and the player turns and runs straight out to catch a ball that the coach tosses over her head. She catches the ball and throws it to the player near the coach. She then runs to her right to catch another tossed ball, which she throws to the player at SS. She then runs to the left to catch a ball tossed to her left; she throws this ball to the fielder playing 2B. She then runs back to the point where she fielded the first ball over her head, and the coach tosses a slow grounder for her to charge, pick up, and run back to the coach. She then takes the place of one of the fielders, and the next player in line steps out.

Variations

You can do this drill with a fly ball over the head followed by a line drive to the left or right or balls over the shoulder to the left and right. This drill can be done in a gym or a small area as long as there's enough room for fielders to use proper technique. The drill can also be done without throws to a receiver, or throws can be to a target if other players aren't available.

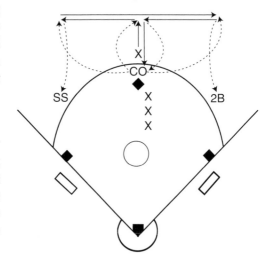

Coaching Points

Make sure players are using proper technique. Hustle is the key. Beating the ball allows the fielder to be more successful. Make sure throws are accurate and that the player always comes back to the point where she made the first catch over her head.

Purpose
To work on speed and getting behind a ground ball to field it properly and make a good throw to a receiver or target

Organization
You need two cones and a coach with a bucket of balls. The coach is at 3B. A single-file line of outfielders is on the left-field sideline. One cone is about 10 feet (3 meters) directly in front of the line of fielders, and the other is 10 feet to the right of the first one.

Execution
The first fielder takes off toward the cone directly in front of her. The coach tosses a ball slightly to the right of the cone so that the fielder goes around the cone before catching it. She returns the ball to the coach (or to a player near the coach who's fielding throws). The fielder then continues to go around the other cone and catches another tossed ball from the coach. She throws it back and jogs back to the end of the line. The next player in line begins. After several repetitions, the line starts on the other side of the cones.

Variations
You can run this drill in a gym or smaller area, and you can go without the throws by the fielder. If you use one cone instead of two, players can stay on that side of the cone and create a new line coming back from the other direction for the next round. You can run this drill with ground balls just as easily as fly balls and line drives.

Coaching Points
Watch for proper footwork. Sprinting to get to the ball and, after the catch, planting to make a balanced, accurate throw is essential.

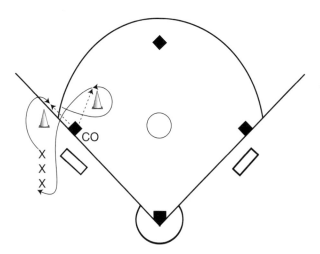

Purpose

To work on playing team defense in the outfield; to practice taking charge and communicating; to learn to recognize who has the best angle for a throw to a base; to train or practice proper back-up technique

Organization

Two lines of fielders stand at centerfield and left field. The coach is behind 2B with a bucket of balls. A fielder is at the 2B position with an empty bucket to receive thrown balls.

Execution

The first players in each line step up. The coach hits or throws a ball in between them, either on the ground or in the air. If the ball is thrown on the ground, one fielder calls for the ball while taking an angle to cut the ball off, while the other fielder becomes a backup. The fielder who fields the ball makes a throw to 2B, simulating an attempt to get a base runner trying to stretch a single into a double. If the ball is thrown in the air, one fielder calls it and simulates throwing to catch a runner tagging up at 1B. Players switch lines after going for the ball or backing up.

Variations

This drill can be done with the fielders in center and right field or just two lines the same distance apart (if space allows) as those in the two outfield positions. The drill can also be run in a gym with less distance between but still using the skills of cutting a ball off, backing up, and getting into proper position to make a throw to a specified receiver or target. If you choose to do fly balls in between, make sure fielders decide who will take the high level and who will take the low level in case they have to dive for the ball.

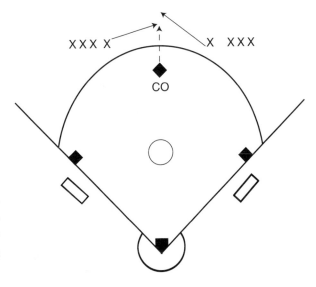

Coaching Points

Communication is key in this drill. Watch for players taking the proper angle to the ball. Getting on balance and making a good throw after changing direction is also important.

BACKUP

Purpose

To work on outfielders making adjustments to the angle and speed of throws to infielders when the outfielder is acting as a backup; to back up outfielders and infielders on hit balls

Organization

Use a standard field setup with a team defense in place. A coach hits situational fungos for players to field. A pitcher pitches balls to the catcher, but these balls are not swung at.

Execution

The coach designates where throws should go when a ball gets hit to each position. The pitcher throws a specific pitch, just as in a game. The coach fungos a ball into the field as though he or she has hit the pitch. The catcher catches the pitch and tosses the ball off to the side, out of the way. If the fungoed ball goes into the outfield, the outfielder purposely misses the ball, and the outfielder backing her up makes the play and throws to the designated location. If the ball gets hit into the infield, the fielder misses the ball purposely, and the outfielder backs her up and makes the play. Subsequent balls hit into the infield will be fielded by the infielder, who throws to the designated base. The receiver intentionally misses the throw, and the backup makes the proper play. If the ball is hit into the outfield, an outfielder fields it and makes a throw to the designated base. Again, the receiver intentionally misses the throw, and the backup (could be an infielder) makes the play.

Variations

You can have as many intentionally missed throws as you like to assess every play that could possibly happen as a backup. You may also add base runners.

Coaching Points

Proper backup procedures can save a game. Stress the recognition of the proper angle to back up and the differences in speed and distance of thrown balls to the bases. The speed of hit balls also needs to be read properly to give the player enough room to be an effective backup.

Purpose

To practice seeing the ball off the bat and getting a good jump on the ball

Organization

Use a standard field setup with one outfielder in each outfield position. You'll need a pitching machine for this drill. No infielders are needed.

Execution

Have hitters take turns hitting sacrifice fly balls off the pitching machine. Outfielders will make the plays and toss caught balls to a shagger behind 2B. The number of repetitions will depend on the number of outfielders available and what they need to work on. After a set number of reps, substitute the first three outfielders with others.

Variations

Add players at 2B and 3B to practice throws with base runners. If you have several outfielders, put two outfielders in each position; whoever gets the best jump on the ball gets to make the play. This makes the drill more competitive. You can also do this drill during live batting practice.

Coaching Points

Emphasize good communication and reading the ball off the bat. Make sure that the outfielder who's not catching the ball becomes a proper backup. Players hustling back into position helps the drill run smoothly. If you add a throw with base runners, the quality of reps is more important than the quantity.

Purpose
To help outfielders get more comfortable playing at or near the fence; to work on preventing balls from going over the fence

Organization
You'll need a bucket of balls. As the drill progresses, a coach and someone to catch throws from a group of outfielders should be included in the setup. Run this drill at the warning track at the fence.

Execution
Each outfielder has a ball for self-toss. Each outfielder finds enough space to self-toss a ball to go for at the fence. After they're comfortable with this, have each outfielder make a self-tossed catch at the fence, one at a time. After they catch their self-toss, they throw to a receiver in a relay position. Now a coach tosses a fly ball to the player close to the fence; she catches it and makes a throw, either to a relay person or to a base. The final progression is to have a coach fungo a fly ball; the fielder catches it, makes a throw, and goes to the end of the line so the next fielder can start.

Variations
On each of the three phases, the player may or may not make a throw. If you want to make sure the fungo balls are consistent, use a machine to shoot the balls to a specific area.

Coaching Points
Plays at the fence don't occur frequently, but when they do occur, the ball must be caught to prevent a big hit. Watch for good communication and field awareness among your outfielders. You might need to make sure fielders are using proper technique before adding balls to the drill. Stress safety—you don't want players getting reckless near the fence.

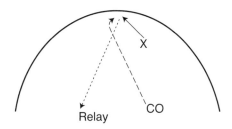

Purpose

To work on using a knee-down and staggered-feet technique for fielding a ground ball, depending on the speed of the ball

Organization

A coach with a bucket of balls either throws or hits ground balls to one fielder at a time. The coach is at 2B; fielders are lined up in centerfield.

Execution

One player steps up and faces the coach. The coach either hits or throws a slow-moving ground ball to the fielder, who uses either a glove-leg forward stagger or a throwing-leg forward stagger to field a slow-moving ground ball and makes a throw back to either the coach or a designated receiver. The fielder then backpedals or sprints back to her original position. The coach now throws or hits a hard ground ball. The fielder uses the "knee down" technique to make sure the ball doesn't get by her; she then makes an easy throw back in to the coach (simulating a situation in which the runner is not advancing). The coach then hits or throws a slow-moving ground ball, and the fielder uses whichever technique they did not use on the first ball to field a slow-mover. She then makes a throw back to 2B. The fielder runs to the end of the line, and the next player begins the drill.

Variations

Draw colored dots on balls to make sure fielders can call out the color as they are fielding the ball; this will encourage the athletes to watch the ball and track it all the way into the glove. The throws can be made to bases other than 2B after fielding the ball. Add runners to the drill if you wish. If you're doing the drill indoors, use softer balls. Eliminate the throws if limited space makes throwing dangerous.

Coaching Points

The outfield is the last line of defense. This drill must be done correctly and intensely. Watching the ball into the glove and the accuracy of the throws can make the difference in whether a runner is safe or out. Use this drill to help your fielders learn to recognize which fielding technique is best for them to use in a given situation.

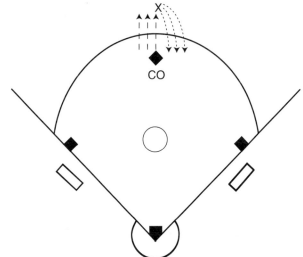

Purpose

To learn to read how a ball will come off a sideline or home run fence and play it appropriately; to work on keeping a runner from advancing an extra base because of a misplayed ball

Organization

You'll need a bucket of balls and two empty buckets. Two lines of outfielders line up in centerfield and left field. A coach has a bucket of balls behind 2B. Players are stationed at 2B and 3B with empty buckets, ready to receive throws from the outfield.

Execution

The first player in each line steps into center and left field positions. The coach hits or throws a ball into the air or on the ground into the left centerfield fence. Both players go for the ball. One calls for the ball while the other communicates where to make the throw. The outfielder who calls for the ball takes the proper angle off the fence to put herself in the best position to make a throw to whatever base the other outfielder has directed her. The fielder makes a throw to that base. After completing the throw, players switch lines so they have the chance to field from both positions.

Variations

This drill can be done with right fielders and centerfielders. Add relay players if you want to work on relay throws. You can also do this drill on a sideline fence (simulating an overthrow from the infield). If you use base runners, make sure the fielders are aware of the speed of the runners. This drill can be done in a gym, using the walls to get an angle. The throws might be shorter, but the footwork and technique are the same.

Coaching Points

Outfielders should focus on clear communication and playing the best angle possible to be on balance for a good throw to the designated base. If using base runners, the fielder not fielding the ball should take a peek at the runner to communicate what base to throw to and get into position to back up the fielder as she fields the ball off the fence.

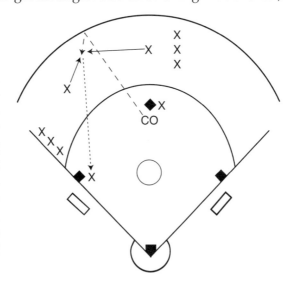

Chapter 11

Pitcher

Kirk Walker Oregon State University Head Coach

Anyone who has played or watched competitive fastpitch softball knows that the pitching position is an important part of the game. Of all players, pitchers have the greatest ability to affect the complexion of a game. Just as in baseball, pitchers are involved in every aspect of the play of the game, yet different from the brother sport of baseball, softball pitchers can throw effectively in multiple games in a day and over several days in a row. This difference is directly related to the position of the arm during the rapid deceleration (sequencing) that results in the release of the pitch. With proper mechanics, fastpitch softball pitchers can stabilize their arm more effectively along the side of the body, thus taxing the rotator cuff muscles to a lesser degree. There are so many different styles of pitching in the sport, and it's imperative that coaches and players alike focus on fundamental mechanics and key principles of pitching. Allow pitchers to find their pitching DNA that gives them their own style. No one can tell a pitcher what her style should be; it's her job to work hard on her mechanics and allow her style to evolve over time.

Most great pitching coaches teach similar things to their pitchers, although the terms they use often vary. Don't place too much importance on pitching style or terms, but instead focus on mechanics and key principles. Key principles of the pitching motion are those important absolutes that all great pitchers share regardless of their size, age, or pitching style. Video analysis provides the opportunity for coaches to stop talking about what they think happens at high speed and actually break down what great pitchers do to be effective, efficient, and successful. Any good pitching drill will work on one or more of the four key principles.

Spacing is a key pitching principle that involves the creation of space alongside the hip for the pitching arm, hand, and ball to move into as the pitcher approaches the release of the pitch. This sounds simple, but one of the most common flaws with young pitchers involves spacing, which is evidenced in accuracy problems from side to side. Spacing also becomes important for the completion of the sequencing principle, which is related to generating power.

Alignment is a key principle that has been taught and stressed by pitching coaches for years. Creating a "power line" or "line of force" with a direct line from the center of the pitching rubber to the center of home plate establishes a clear reference point. Keeping the arm circle, leg stride, and follow-through in alignment with the line of force increases success and maximizes efficiency. Any time a pitcher moves a body part away from the line of force, additional energy is required to compensate or correct, which is inefficient to the pitching motion.

Sequencing is a key principle best described as the creation of a whip with the arm as the pitcher moves into her release. Sequencing translates the maximum amount of energy created in the body and arm into the ball on release. Sequencing begins at foot touch, which rapidly slows the linear movement of the body. As the arm is approaching the third quarter of the circle, the elbow should lead, with the ball and hand lagging behind. The rapid deceleration of the upper arm alongside the body during stabilization just prior to release causes a rapid acceleration or whipping of the ball and pitching hand forward past the center of mass of the body. Last, the elbow and upper arm are released from stabilization and allowed to move forward down the power line, thereby releasing the stress in the shoulder and arm created during release of the ball.

Posturing is an important pitching principle stressed in several drills in this chapter. Good posturing, as seen in all great pitchers, goes through three distinct positions during the fastpitch motion. Initial *attack* posture is created when the pitcher bends at the knees and leans her whole body forward, with head and shoulders moving forward of the hips. This occurs early in the motion before the start of the pitching circle. *Reversed* posture occurs in all great pitchers between the first quarter of the arm circle and circle peak. This reversal of posture can be seen with the hips moving forward of the head and shoulders. You can see this in a leaning back of the upper body at circle peak. This position at circle peak is often called the "X" or "K" position because of the relationship of the arms and legs when the body is sideways. Finally, *upright* posture occurs just prior to release of the pitch and should bring the pitcher's posture back to a more upright position, allowing for greater accuracy of the pitch.

All of the drills in this chapter emphasize aspects of one or more of the key principles. Many drills help a pitcher with more than one principle at a time. It is important that all levels of pitchers understand the key principles so that the drills will have more purpose during execution.

RESISTANCE

Purpose

To teach the concept of resistance for the pitcher

Organization

The pitcher, wearing her glove, should place her stride leg (glove leg) forward and at a 45-degree angle, with her foot placed up against the fence or wall. The pitching leg (drag leg) should be back behind the front leg about three to four feet (.9 to 1.2 meters). This sideways position is similar to the position a pitcher will be in at foot touch. The pitcher should be perpendicular to the wall or fence.

Execution

The pitcher drags her back leg forward toward the front leg, making a figure 4, with the calf of the drag leg coming close to the back of the front knee. As the pitcher is dragging, she'll be pushing and resisting back away from the fence or wall. The front leg should not be locked out but should be firm and strong so that the forward movement can be resisted. Once the pitcher drags to her figure-4 position, she pushes back against the fence with her front leg, which causes her to step back to her original position. This action can be done repeatedly. When doing this drill against a fence, the upper body arm circle or swing should not be added; this will prevent the hand from hitting the fence.

Variations

Using a curb, step, or even a base can work to create an object to block against and help simulate resistance; this might also allow for a full arm circle to be incorporated. The pitcher should remain on the dirt so that the dragging action simulates a gamelike scenario and feel.

Coaching Points

Proper lower body execution helps to maintain spacing and adds into sequencing with the upper body. The dragging and resistance will be important to a pitcher's ability to bring her body back to an upright posture prior to release. Dragging and resistance help with both sequencing and posturing.

Purpose

To isolate the lower body and focus on the upper body, arm circle, sequencing, spacing, release posture, elbow release, and follow-through

Organization

The pitcher needs a bucket of pitching balls and a catch net set up behind home plate, or she can use a single ball and a catcher. Draw a power line or line of force that travels from the center of the pitching rubber through the center tip of home plate. The pitcher should stand 15 to 20 feet (4.5 to 6 meters) from the target or catcher.

Execution

The pitcher kneels down on the knee of her back leg (pitching leg) so that the knee is directly on the line. She places the foot of her front leg (glove leg) on the power line so that the front leg is slightly bent. She begins this drill with her glove and pitching hands together alongside her pitching leg. She needs to make sure that she's rounding her back so that her shoulders are across the power line. This creates and maintains good spacing for the pitching arm on completion of the arm circle. She begins with her glove arm and pitching arm moving forward together without separating until after the pitching arm has passed the first quarter of the arm circle. The arm should be relaxed and loose, not locked out. The pitcher continues around, focusing on a good release directly down the line of force.

Variations

Do this drill with a weighted ball (but use caution not to overthrow). This setup can also work well for rise ball spins.

Coaching Points

As the arm continues up to circle peak it should remain on that imaginary line of force. Don't allow the pitcher to arch her back and swing her pitching arm behind her head. The finish of the arm circle is important when working on this drill. The proper posture is for the pitcher's shoulders to remain over her hips; she should not allow them to lean forward or back. A firm wrist on release allows for maximum transfer of the arm sequencing into the linear speed of the ball. Pitchers do not need to throw strikes during this drill as long as the ball remains over the power line. In other words, make sure the pitch stays straight and does not miss inside or outside of the plate. Key principles to emphasize in this drill are sequencing, spacing, and alignment.

Purpose

To highlight and focus on proper arm sequence from foot touch into release by isolating the body position and posture

Organization

Position the pitcher on the power line about 20 to 25 feet (6 to 7.6 meters) from a target catch net (or catcher). The feet should be 3 to 5 feet (.9 to 1.5 meters) apart, depending on the size of the pitcher. The glove arm will be extended forward toward the target or catcher, and the pitching arm should reach back away from the target, making the letter X or K position with the body. The toes should be on the power line, and the shoulders should lean over the toes or beyond to create spacing (*a*). A reversed body posture position should be created by the back shoulder being behind the back hip, which makes the body look like it is leaning back toward 2B. The glove should be toward the target and pitching hand, palm facing away.

Execution

From the proper foot-touch position just described, the pitcher should begin the pitching arm moving forward by focusing on leading with the back elbow and allowing the ball and pitching hand to lag behind (*b*). The pitching arm should move alongside the upper body in the spacing created by the pitcher. As the upper arm stabilizes along the upper body, the pitching hand whips or sequences forward past the center of mass. After release of the pitch, the upper arm and elbow are released from their stabilized positions and move slightly away from the body and continue forward down the power line to the finish position. The lower body will work simultaneously with the arm swing. The drag leg or pitching leg will continue to drag forward, helping to accelerate the arm into stabilization and then rapid deceleration along the side of the body.

Coaching Points

Because of the lack of forward or linear movement, this drill should be done very relaxed with little emphasis on generating speed. Teaching the proper sequencing principle eventually leads to maximum power generation with the most efficient transfer. Always stress the importance of alignment with the line of force or power line. If a pitcher does miss the strike zone, it should be either lower or higher but not side to side. Strikes are not the most important measure of success for most progression drills. In addition to sequencing, alignment, and the finish upright posturing position, the key principle of spacing should be maintained throughout the drill.

Purpose

To help train the pitcher in the reversal of posture as she enters circle peak

Organization

The pitcher can stand either on the pitching rubber with her pivot foot on the front edge of the center of the pitching rubber or on the power line. She should have a ball in her hand. She takes position with her pivot foot on the power line and the glove knee lifted up at 90 degrees. The pitching hand, ball, and glove should be together, with both arms facing the plate at the first quarter of the pitching motion. This is what appears to be a standing crane (a).

Execution

The pitcher lifts up with the pitching arm, glove arm, and glove leg straight up toward the circle peak position. As she makes this move she'll stand up on her pivot toe and twist sideways, with her pitching arm and glove arm separating as her hips turn sideways (b). She won't drive forward toward the catcher, but her glove leg and arm will pivot and reach toward the catcher as the pitching arm reaches back toward 2B. The pitcher should be tall but keep her abs tight and shoulders over her toes. From this split sideways position, she should just let her front foot and leg drop down so they land toe to toe on the power line. She should land in a good foot-touch position with shoulders over toes, creating spacing.

Variations

This drill can be done without throwing a pitch toward a net or target. Once the pitcher has mastered the skill, she can continue from foot touch into release. You can move the distance progressively back to almost a full pitching distance.

Coaching Points

This is a drill to work on the pivot of the drag foot, the splitting of the arms, and the reversal of posture. This drill does not incorporate the forward linear movement yet but is an important step in learning posturing. Make sure the pitcher doesn't drop her arms and leg down before the upward movement and split. Coaches should look for pitchers leaning or arching their backs because this makes creating spacing on the foot touch more difficult. Learning to reverse posture is an important concept that all great pitchers accomplish.

Purpose
To focus on forward movement of the body prior to foot touch

Organization
The pitcher should stand on the power line about 25 to 30 feet (7.6 to 9 meters) from home plate or the target. The pitcher needs either a bucket of balls and a catch net or a ball and a catcher at home plate.

Execution
The pitcher stands with both feet together on the power line with toes and hips turned sideways so that the glove hip and shoulder face the target (or catcher). With the glove hand and pitching hand together next to the pitching leg, the pitcher rounds her shoulders, creating space, before moving forward. Her pitching shoulder should be over her toes throughout her arm circle to allow for proper spacing along her pitching leg for her pitching arm to get into prior to release (a). The pitcher loads onto her pitching leg and creates an attack posture by leaning toward the target (or catcher) prior to her arms moving. The pitching arm, glove arm, and stride leg should move forward down the power line together. As her arms move past the first quarter of the arm circle, her hands begin to split and she moves into foot-touch position (b). At first she should stop in sideways or X position at foot touch. If she has landed at foot touch in the proper position, the remainder of the arm circle and release can occur. After a few repetitions of stopping in foot-touch position and then continuing, she can move continuously into release without stopping to check the position at foot touch. With the addition of the linear movement forward into the pitching, it becomes important to make sure that the pitcher creates some resistance in her front leg as the sequencing begins at foot touch.

Coaching Points
The first part of this drill is important in teaching attack posture into a reversed posture at foot touch. Look for the reversal of posture position when landing at foot touch. The pitcher's position at foot touch should be checked before allowing her to move forward into release. To maintain good spacing at foot touch, some pitchers are aided by thinking about keeping their stomach or abdominal muscles tight. The front foot should land at about a 45-degree angle. Toes should both be on the power line. When having pitchers move directly through foot touch without the pause, keep an eye on good mechanics; if they fall short, step back to the pause at foot touch. With the increased forward or linear movement it's important to see the pitcher begin resisting or firming her front leg on foot touch to begin sequencing. Additionally, leg drag along with the arm swing should help translate power to the ball.

Purpose
To work on using the entire body to maximize the leg drive off the mound

Organization
The pitcher has a ball and glove and uses a permanent pitching rubber.

Execution
The first progression starts with a basic standing broad jump *(a)* with no glove, swinging arms, loading legs, and jumping both feet as far as possible *(b)*. The second progression is a standing broad jump with no glove and jumping with only the pitching leg *(c)* while the other leg swings *(d)*. The third progression is with the glove on *(e)*, striding out with only the glove leg and driving out to the X position while dragging the pitching foot away from the pitching rubber *(f)*. Adding in full motion with glove on but no ball in hand, work on striding out as far as possible while still being able to be legal, and drag the pitching foot away from the pitching rubber. The fourth progression adds in the ball but without throwing the pitch.

Variations
Pitchers can mark their own distances and see if they can get stronger each day. They can add to their stride length without worrying about throwing a pitch.

Coaching Points
Use the standing broad jump to help pitchers learn how to use their arms, legs, and body lean to help drive off the pitching rubber. Once the pitcher is simulating her pitching motion, make sure that she works on being aggressive

but remains legal by keeping her drag foot in contact with the ground. The better that pitchers can use their legs, pitching arm, and glove arm together, the greater distance they'll be able to legally travel away from the pitching rubber. Although increasing stride length is beneficial in strengthening a pitcher's legs, there will be a point at which stride length won't add to power generation because it will affect posture and sequencing capabilities.

Purpose

To work on the pitcher using leg drive off the mound and understanding attack posture

Organization

Use a normal pitching workout area. The pitcher needs either a bucket of balls and a sock net at the catching target area or a catcher and a few balls.

Execution

The pitcher takes position on the pitching rubber with a single ball in her pitching hand. She stands with her pivot foot on the pitching rubber at the center and with the ball of her foot just over the front edge of the plate. She swings her pitching arm with the ball, her glove arm with her glove on, and her glove leg all together forward (a) and back (b). This movement requires balance as she completes two swings forward and back with her arms and legs. On the third swing forward, she'll use the momentum of her arm and leg swing with a really aggressive attack posture or body lean forward just prior to driving out and away from the pitching rubber. She should remain legal and in contact with the ground while driving toward home plate and down the power line. After pitchers land aggressively down the power line, they'll continue with good mechanics and finish the pitch.

Variations

This drill can be done at first without the ball and then with the ball. The drill can also be done with or without the ball, but stop in foot-touch position to check on spacing and posture principles.

Coaching Points

Make sure that proper mechanics are used when the pitcher attempts to maximize her leg drive and push off the mound. Teaching points for the posturing principle occur with the attack position just prior to driving off the pitching rubber, the reversal of posture between first quarter and circle peak that's evident at foot touch, and bringing the posture back to an upright position prior to release. It's important to allow her pitching arm to go along for the ride and not to force arm speed. At foot touch, check on her spacing and her ability to sequence with the increased power from the leg drive.

Purpose

To gain rhythm in the pitching motion off the rubber; to increase the aggressive leg drive pitchers should use toward home plate

Organization

Draw a power line from the pitching rubber toward home plate about 10 feet (3 meters) in length. You can do this drill with a bucket of pitching balls and a catch net or with a catcher.

Execution

The pitcher begins by starting with her stride foot behind the rubber and her pivot (pitching) foot a step behind her stride foot. As she steps forward and onto the pitching rubber with her pivot, or pitching, foot, she begins to aggressively load onto her pitching leg and lean forward into her attack posture. The glove and pitching hand should come together just to the side of the hip. With an aggressive stride down the power line the pitcher will move her stride leg, pitching arm, and glove arm all together toward the first quarter of the arm circle. The pitch should be finished with aggressive leg drive, resistance, finish, and follow-through.

Variations

Do this drill at a slightly longer distance to increase leg strength. The drill can also be done as a power drill at a very close distance while throwing into a fence or catch net.

Coaching Points

This is a great drill for rhythm, getting the pitcher to use her entire body effortlessly. Good mechanics at all of the key points is important, and the key principles of posturing, spacing, sequencing, and alignment should always be stressed.

Purpose

To help pitchers incorporate leg strength; to help pitchers rely on their legs more than just their arm speed; to expose flaws a pitcher has with alignment

Organization

This drill doesn't require a pitching mound and is often done from deep beyond the mound. A catcher and a bucket of balls is preferred, although you can use a catch net with a backstop if no catcher is available.

Execution

Starting near 2B, the pitcher uses a walk-through approach to use her legs. As she walks into throwing the ball, her main focus shouldn't be on throwing hard but on launching the ball high into the air to create a high arc. The goal is to reach the catcher or net on the fly, with no bounces. With each release or toss, the pitcher should take a few steps back away from home plate, adding to the distance. The greater the distance she moves back, the greater the arc the ball should be thrown with to the catcher.

Coaching Points

The greater the distance, the more small errors are exaggerated. Pitchers will make great improvements in distance as long as they are throwing with their legs. The pitcher should not appear to use a fast arm circle or look like she's pitching with her normal motion. She'll keep her glove and pitching hand in front of her hip so that her stride leg and both arms move forward together. Make sure that she's using an aggressive leg drag and keeping her body in a reversed posture position into release instead of bringing her posture back to an upright position on release.

Purpose

To help break a pitcher from a tendency to walk through her resistance

Organization

This drill is done with the pitcher in her normal pitching workout area with a pitching rubber and a home plate. You'll need a cardboard box or shoe box, which is placed directly in front of the pitcher's pitching leg in the finish position. This spot will be next to where the stride foot lands at foot touch but in front of the pitching foot position. The box should be empty in case the pitcher walks past her stride foot and makes contact or kicks the box. The placement of the box needs to be based on a full aggressive pitch.

Execution

The pitcher throws any pitch of her choice. As she finishes the pitch (close to but behind the box), she'll get feedback on whether she has resisted enough to stop her forward progress. If the box is kicked or moved, replace the box and make adjustments for the next pitch. Proper lower body execution will help maintain spacing and add to proper sequencing with the upper body. Finally, the dragging and resistance are important in bringing her body back to an upright posture prior to release.

Coaching Points

Placing a box in front of the pitcher's stride leg provides an obstacle that she'll need to stay behind when finishing her pitch. Coaching feedback is minimized because the pitcher receives immediate feedback from the box. Resistance is an important component to sequencing and posturing, and the pitcher must make sure she doesn't change her motion just to avoid contact with the box. Some pitchers will step wide of the box to avoid contact but will still be walking through resistance. If this occurs, adjust the box location to minimize this problem.

DRAG OBSTACLE KICK

Purpose

To place an object (box) in proper position for the pitcher to drag her pitching leg into a figure-4 position; to work on increasing aggressive leg dragging and proper positioning of the figure 4

Organization

This drill is done with the pitcher in her normal pitching workout area with a pitching rubber and a home plate. You'll need a cardboard box or shoe box, the placement of which is determined by the pitcher's stride leg. The box should be placed just behind the back heel of the plant foot at foot touch. Be careful not to place the box so close that the pitcher contacts it with her plant foot. With a few repetitions you'll be able to adjust the box to the correct placement.

Execution

The pitcher throws a pitch that includes dragging her pitching leg into a figure-4 position. As she completes the pitch, she should make contact with the box with the side of her drag foot as she gets close to the figure-4 position.

Variations

You can combine this drill with the previous drill (Box Resistance) or with any drill that requires a pitcher to drag into figure-4 position. For additional feedback, this drill can be set up when pitchers are working on moving pitches.

Coaching Points

Whether she contacts the box or not, the pitcher gets immediate feedback. Pitchers should always work on throwing aggressively and with proper mechanics without thinking about the box. Figure-4 position is attained when the drag foot lifts off the ground at the completion of the drag and the shin or calf gets very close to the back of the knee of the plant leg. The numeral 4 can be seen in the leg position when you're looking at the pitcher from the catching position.

Purpose

To help pitchers feel the concept of spacing and sequencing

Organization

All you need is a miniature or foam football. The pitcher stands anywhere from 30 to 50 feet (9 to 15 meters) from another pitcher or a catcher.

Execution

The pitcher pitches the football using her full circle motion. She should grip the football with her fingers on the seam but near the back tip of the ball. (She can fine-tune her finger placement with repetitions and experience.) The object is to create spacing and use sequencing to throw the football with a spiral to the catcher.

Variations

As pitchers become more competent, increase the size and weight of the football and the distance the ball is thrown.

Coaching Points

This is a great warm-up or cool-down drill. The feedback of the spiral (or lack of spiral) helps the pitcher make adjustments. This drill is good for working on the rise ball spins as well as fastball mechanics and the principles of spacing and sequencing.

135 TARGET TOSS

Purpose
To challenge advanced pitchers on their location and control

Organization
Ideally, this drill is done without a catcher but in a place that allows a full pitching distance. Use a catch net with targets taped off or small pieces of material placed onto the netting. There are some very good products on the market, including The Zone In, that allow for very specific pitching zones to be set up and altered quickly and easily. Here you would like to be able to isolate the four corners of the strike zone and, for younger pitchers, a fifth zone in the center of the strike zone.

Execution
The coach or pitcher should call out the location to be worked on. As the pitcher goes through her normal pitch she'll key on the specific zone and attempt to hit that spot. If she succeeds, then move on to a different zone. If she fails, she should be given a second or third attempt. The additional attempts should be eliminated as the pitcher becomes more and more competent.

Coaching Points
This drill becomes more and more useful as pitchers get closer to games. It is important to do some target work without a catcher or an umpire calling balls and strikes. To maximize control components and body adjustments, pitchers sometimes need to learn to throw pitches that are not always inside the strike zone. It is important to learn how to set up a hitter and get her to chase pitches in locations outside of the strike zone as well.

Purpose

To promote better understanding of the spin and movement of certain pitches and how to create greater ball movement at the most important time

Organization

Pitchers need a glove and will throw from a pitching mound. This drill can be done with or without a catcher. You'll need two batting tees and a medium- to light-weight string or stretchy cord about four to five feet (1.2 to 1.5 meters) long. If the drill is done without a catcher, you'll also need a catch net and a bucket of balls. If using a catcher, the catcher or coach should be in full catching gear for maximum safety.

Execution

Place tees in the front of the batter's box on each side of home plate. The string or stretchy cord should be fashioned with a loop on both ends large enough to slide over the tee top. Adjust the height of the string to the top of the knee caps for a typical batter you're working with. The pitcher will work on throwing a drop ball that travels over the top of the string and is caught by the catcher (or in the sock net) as low to the ground as possible.

Variations

The height of the string can be altered for pitches other than the drop ball. For example, if working on the rise ball, the string can be raised to the top of the strike zone with additional buckets placed under the tees. For pitchers struggling with throwing their fastball consistently too high in the zone, a second string can be placed belt high, thus shrinking the zone and raising the demand placed on the pitcher.

Coaching Points

A visual measure helps to create a better understanding of the spin and movement of certain pitchers as well as how to create greater ball movement at the most important time. The string (or another visual target) takes much of the pressure off the coach or catcher in giving feedback to the pitcher. The string becomes a feedback system that validates quality pitches. Pitchers should not ease up to work only on their control but should throw at gamelike intensity.

Chapter 12

Catcher

Kelly Inouye-Perez   UCLA Head Coach

Many coaches consider the catching position to be the most important position in fastpitch softball. The catcher is the only player with a complete view of the field of play on defense. The catcher must possess knowledge of the game, solid physical mechanics, and a great relationship with her pitcher and teammates. A solid catcher behind the plate is like having a coach on the field. There's a saying in softball I'm sure you've heard: "Great defense wins championships." A solid defense can stop even the most feared offense any day of the week.

For every team the key to success starts with the pitcher in the circle. And behind every great pitcher is a catcher who can make her better. Some coaches call the catcher the team's quarterback. The catcher calls pitches, communicates defensive plays, and even calls time-out to control the tempo of the game. For the catcher to help her pitcher, she must exude confidence in her demeanor and physical play. For a catcher to exude confidence, she must practice her physical skills as much as a pitcher practices her pitches.

Many coaches set up practice with infield ground balls, outfield groundballs and pop flies, pitcher workouts, and batting practice. That's a general template for most teams. Because of time constraints, field availability, or lack of enough staff to train the catchers, few practices include drills to improve the catcher's physical play. Coaches sometimes forget that aside from the pitcher, the catcher touches the ball more than any other player in the game. All the plays the catcher is involved in are game-changing plays, including attempted steals, passed balls, sacrifice bunts, and plays at the plate. But how often do coaches practice these critical plays?

The physical skills of a catcher must be perfected so that she can "think the game" for the team and not worry about the physical demands of the position. This only comes with dedicated practice of the physical game behind the plate.

A common weakness among catchers is the inability to keep a ball pitched in the dirt in front of their bodies. Some catchers love to block, and some dread it. Some catchers become excited when the ball is in the dirt and try to "save the play" by picking the ball in the dirt with their glove and coming up with the ball to throw the runner out. It looks great when played out perfectly, but catchers might admit that this play was more luck than skill. Instead, this lazy mentality of trying to catch the ball with just the glove—"picking it"—often makes a play worse because the ball hits the glove in motion and rolls away from the catcher, which allows the runner to advance easily. Practicing proper blocking technique (using the body to keep the ball in front) can make a huge difference in a game. It gives the pitcher confidence and tells opponents they have to work a lot harder at advancing the runner.

Another common weakness behind the plate is the errant throw to second base. It seems that Monday through Friday the throw is quite accurate but in a game, very inconsistent. Any catcher can tell you that accuracy is all about the grip on the ball. This grip is accomplished with a consistent transition from receiving the ball and transitioning to throw. How often do coaches practice this transition? Well, you might say every time they throw to second base, but how often do you have a gamelike runner stealing second for each of your catchers to get their throws in at practice? The Transition Drill will help improve consistency in your catcher's throws. Once her transition is smooth, she won't have a need to rush her throws.

How about the play at the plate? Everyone holds their breath as they watch this play develop, but how often do they practice it in practice with a live runner coming into the catcher to make the play gamelike? The Play at the Plate drill can help your catcher prepare for big plays at the plate.

One of the worst plays to watch is a catcher stumbling underneath a high foul pop-up and then dropping it. This is a case of a missed out that often comes back to bite you. Catchers should practice pop flies as much as infielders practice ground balls. No pop fly is the same, but with enough practice they become routine outs.

In this chapter are 12 drills that every catcher should practice and perfect to gain the confidence she needs to play the position. Catcher is an important position with a lot of responsibility and can also be an enjoyable position to play.

Purpose

To practice correct technique in blocking balls in the dirt

Organization

The catcher is in full gear behind home plate. You'll need paddles for both hands for this drill. Use softie balls to avoid fear of getting hit by the ball. The coach stands in front of the plate to throw balls at the catcher.

Execution

Body blow (pictured). Start the catcher on her knees in correct blocking position: forward lean, rounded shoulders, tucked chin. Paddles are touching the ground; both palms are facing the coach. The coach throws short hops at the catcher so that the balls bounce into the catcher's chest. Catchers should focus on using the center of the chest protector to block the ball down toward home plate. This allows them to use the body, not the paddles, to block the ball. The paddles touch the ground to prevent the ball from going through her legs.
From the squat. The catcher is in her squat position. The coach throws short hops into the catcher's chest, focusing on blocking down toward the plate. The paddles touch the ground to prevent the ball from passing through her legs.

Variations

If you don't have paddles, use bare hands. Be sure the catcher has open palms facing the coach to block the ball from going through her legs (might prevent a broken finger). You can use tennis balls for this drill and go without the paddles.

Coaching Points

The focus of this drill is to use the body to block in correct position. The focus should be to block the ball with the center of the chest, not the glove. Focus on blocking with the logo on the center of the chest on the chest protector. The glove is taken away so that the catcher doesn't try to pick the ball with her glove. The paddles (or glove) are allowed to go up no higher than the belly button while the catcher keeps her open palms facing the ball. The paddle (glove) is used only to block balls from going through the legs. Progress to using the glove and real balls.

Purpose

To practice blocking the ball in the dirt laterally

Organization

A catcher in full gear stands behind the plate facing a coach with three balls in his or her hand. The catcher can use paddles to focus on blocking with the body or use her glove.

Execution

The catcher blocks three consecutive balls while moving in one lateral direction. On the coach's command, the catcher begins moving laterally in the direction indicated by the coach. The coach throws an overhand throw at the catcher, which simulates a lateral ball in the dirt. The catcher must block and get up into the catching position as quickly as possible to get ready to block the next ball. The drill is done correctly if the catcher keeps all three balls in front of her.

Variations

Vary the number of balls thrown at the catcher. Vary the speed of how quickly you throw the balls consecutively. Vary how much ground the catcher must cover.

Coaching Points

This drill simulates how quickly a catcher must block and then get back up to be ready to throw the ball. It also builds strength in the catcher's legs. To keep the drill moving, the coach starts with three balls in his or her hands. It's important for the coach to feed an overhand short hop that leads the catcher laterally on the go. You need open space to perform this drill because you don't want the catcher to run into anything. The farther the catcher travels, the stronger her legs will be, and she'll be able to cover a wider range behind the plate.

PLAY AT THE PLATE

Purpose

To practice receiving balls from the outfield for a play at the plate with a runner in motion at the plate

Organization

A catcher in full gear stands at the plate. You need an exercise ball to start up the third-base line to roll toward the catcher to simulate a runner in motion. You need a coach hitting fungos from various outfield positions to simulate an outfielder's throw home.

Execution

As a coach hits a fungo from an outfield position, have someone roll the exercise ball toward the catcher to simulate the runner in motion. The catcher must focus on catching the ball first (a) and then applying the tag to the "runner" (b). If there's limited space, have a coach throw balls from different outfield positions.

Variations

Roll the exercise ball at the catcher to focus on receiving the ball with the runner making contact with the catcher. Vary the angle of the fungo to simulate throws from all outfield positions. Practice applying a tag toward the plate to a runner who slides into the back side of the plate to avoid the tag.

Coaching Points

This drill helps ensure that the catcher doesn't get in the runner's lane too early or too late to block. This will practice the gamelike action of a play at the plate. It's good practice for timing and positioning of the catcher.

Purpose
To work on improving the catcher's first step out of the shoot by forcing her to stay low and drive forward

Organization
A catcher in full gear lies on her belly about three feet (one meter) behind the plate. Her head is closest to the plate. The coach sets a ball out in front of the plate for the catcher to field (*a*).

Execution
The catcher waits to hear the coach say, "Go!" and then uses her legs to drive forward (like a track start) off the ground out toward the ball (*b*). The catcher focuses on staying low and using her legs to get a good jump out of the shoot to field the bunt.

Variations
Place balls in different locations to practice correct footwork on all bunts. Time the catcher to field a certain amount of bunts within a set time. Place a hand about four feet (1.2 meters) above the catcher to challenge her to stay low while driving out of the shoot.

Coaching Points
Be sure the catcher is under control while driving forward so that she can decelerate before fielding the ball. The ball should be fielded out in front of the back foot (not in between the catcher's legs). Be sure the catcher sets up with proper footwork (feet in line with the base she's throwing to) while fielding the ball.

Purpose
To practice getting a good grip on the ball while fielding the bunt

Organization
A catcher is in full gear behind the plate. Put six balls in a straight line about four feet (1.2 meters) apart and about five feet (1.5 meters) in front of the catcher.

Execution
The catcher waits to hear the coach say, "Go!" and then runs to field one ball at a time by setting up her feet to align with the base she's throwing to. The catcher travels up the line of balls while practicing proper footwork and fielding the ball with two hands. After fielding all the balls, the catcher returns to her starting point.

Variations
Place balls in different locations to practice correct footwork on all bunts to all bases. Set balls up the 3B line and have the catcher work on fielding the ball with her back to the infield and spinning to throw the ball to 1B. Time the catcher to practice gamelike speed.

Coaching Points
This drill works on improving quickness to the ball and proper footwork. The catcher should get around the ball to align her feet to the base she's throwing to. She will field the ball and transition to a throwing motion and then place the ball back down on the ground before moving to the next ball. She should field the bunt out in front of her back foot to be able to load weight on her back foot and then throw to the base. She should focus on getting a good grip on the ball while staying low and balanced. If she has time she can shuffle her feet toward the base to make a strong throw. The throw to 1B should always be to the inside of the bag to avoid throwing the ball in the running lane.

Purpose

To practice receiving the ball and getting a good grip while transitioning to throw

Organization

A catcher is in full gear behind the plate. A pitching machine is on the pitching rubber. A coach feeds balls into the machine.

Execution

Set the machine to the same speed as your pitcher. Feed a ball into the machine. The catcher receives the ball and practices getting a good grip on the ball while transitioning to throw. Using a machine allows the catcher to get a lot of balls. Eventually progress to a live pitcher throwing to the catcher.

Variations

Vary the height and speed of the pitch. Have the catcher throw the ball to bases to simulate the steal or pick-off.

Coaching Points

The key to a good throw is a good grip on the ball. The catcher should always try to get a grip across the ball's horseshoe seam. Catchers should try to throw the ball with a spin that moves from 12 o'clock to 6 o'clock, which allows for a straight throw to the base. A throw with bad spin travels to the left or to the right of the base, which makes it difficult for the receiving player. The player receiving the throw already has the sliding runner as a distraction, so the throw must be accurate to allow for an easier play at the base.

The catcher should try to transition from catching the ball in her throwing hand out in front of her body. This allows her more time to get a good grip on the ball. She should have her throwing hand close to her glove to allow a quicker transition. Her throwing hand can follow her glove behind her glove fingers to avoid getting hit by the pitched ball.

Purpose

To practice throwing to a moving target (on the run) such as occurs on steals or pick-offs

Organization

A catcher stands in full gear behind the plate. Two players start at 1B ready to receive the throw from the catcher while running toward 2B. The fielders at 1B each start with a ball.

Execution

The player at 1B throws the ball to the catcher who's standing behind home plate. The player at 1B starts to run toward 2B. The catcher leads the player on the run by throwing the ball in front of the player running toward 2B. This practices the timing and location of throwing to a moving target.

Variations

Start players at 2B running toward 3B or players at 2B running toward 1B.

Coaching Points

This drill helps practice pick-off plays or bunt plays in which the fielder isn't at the base but on the run. The catcher shouldn't wait for the fielder to get to the base. The catcher should lead the fielder with the throw so the fielder doesn't have to stop running. The throw should be waist high so the fielder doesn't have to slow down to receive the ball.

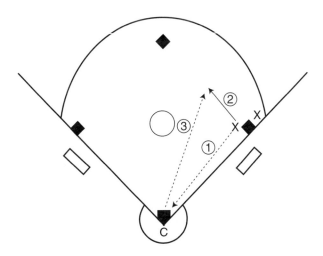

Purpose

To practice proper mechanics of catching the foul ball pop fly

Organization

A catcher stands in full gear behind home plate. A pitching machine is on the plate facing the field. A coach feeds balls into the machine.

Execution

The coach aims the pitching machine up in the air to simulate a foul ball. The catcher starts in a squat with eyes closed. The coach puts a ball in the machine and says, "Go!" The catcher stands up and turns around with her back to the infield to receive the pop fly. She should run under the ball to receive it out in front of her forehead.

Variations

Vary the height or location of the pop fly.

Coaching Points

The ball close to the backstop is easiest to receive if the catcher runs to the backstop and then pulls off the backstop to receive the ball. The catcher should go to the fence with an open palm to the fence to avoid hurting her fingers. She should always catch the ball with two hands to keep the spinning ball from popping out of the catcher's glove. The catcher should "give" with the ball to catch it with soft hands.

Purpose

To practice accuracy and a soft touch to toss the ball to the pitcher on a passed ball or wild pitch at the plate

Organization

The catcher is in full gear. You'll need a backstop or wall to bounce a ball against, a bucket of balls, and a receiver to catch the ball at home plate.

Execution

Have the catcher toss a ball off the wall (to simulate a wild pitch) and then catch it and turn around to toss the ball to the receiver at home plate. The catcher should stay low and keep a short backswing on the underhand toss to the plate to allow for a soft touch to the toss. She should keep a straight arm (locked at the elbow) to avoid tossing the ball over the receiver's head. The throw should be about waist high to the receiver, which allows for an easier play at the plate.

Variations

The catcher can toss the ball in different locations to practice various wild pitches and their bounces. Vary the distance of the wall or backstop to prepare for various backstop depths at various fields.

Coaching Points

This is a toss that needs to be practiced because it can turn a bad play (passed ball or wild pitch) into an out at the plate. It's a tough play that requires accurate location and good speed on the toss to allow the pitcher to easily catch the ball and tag the runner sliding into the plate. This is a play used on a backstop that's close to the plate or for a ball that bounces off the backstop and is close to the plate.

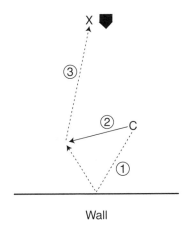

Wall

Purpose
To improve the quickness of the throw from home to 2B

Organization
A catcher is in full gear behind home plate. A fielder receives the ball at 2B. A pitching machine is on the mound facing the plate. A coach feeds balls into the machine. Use a stopwatch to time the throw to 2B.

Execution
A coach pitches a ball to the catcher while a second coach times the throw to 2B. The stopwatch starts when the pitched ball touches the glove of the catcher and stops when the ball touches the glove of the fielder who receives the ball at 2B. This determines a true glove-to-glove time. The goal is to get the throw to 2B in less than two seconds.

Variations
Vary the location of the pitch to make the throw more gamelike. Vary the speed of the machine to simulate different pitches.

Coaching Points
This drill shows a catcher that a quick and accurate throw is more effective than loading up and throwing as hard as she can. The catcher works to improve the quickness of her throw by trying to beat the clock. She should focus on keeping her throwing hand as close to her glove as possible to allow for a quick transition to her throw. She should be short and compact; her throw's power should come from her legs, torso, and wrist snap.

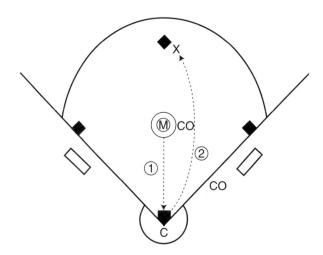

Purpose

To allow catchers to get many different types of throws within a short time

Organization

You'll need a regulation field setup, an extra home plate, and a portable throw base. You'll need two pitchers to pitch to the catchers and an infielder at each base to receive throws. Place one catcher behind the primary, permanent home plate. Place the throw home plate about 10 feet (3 meters) to the 3B side of home, with a catcher behind it. A pitcher stands on the permanent pitcher's mound and throws to the catcher behind the primary home plate. The second pitcher stands about 10 feet to the side of the primary pitching rubber at the same distance and throws to the catcher behind the throw plate. Place the throw base 10 feet to the side of 2B on the 3B side. Make sure that the distance between home and 2B is equal for both the temporary and permanent setups. Halfway through the drill you'll use the same setup but to the 1B side of home plate, pitcher's mound, and 2B. Give pitchers a bucket of balls each in case of bad throws, or have them receive the ball back from the base that the catcher throws to.

Execution

Pitchers each throw pitches to their catcher. If you have two catchers, have them stay at the same home plate for a set number of throws. If you have more than two catchers, have them rotate back and forth every two to three throws. For the first round, catchers on the 3B side work on straight steal throws to the throw base with the SS covering. The catcher behind the permanent plate works on pick-offs to 1B with either the second baseman or first baseman covering. Make sure all catchers rotate to both stations to get their set of throws.

The second round will have the throw base, plate, and pitching area set up on the 1B side. The temporary side works on steal throws with either the SS or second baseman covering. The permanent plate catchers throw pick-offs and steal throws to 3B with the third baseman and SS covering.

Variations

Eliminate the defenders and place buckets on the bases for the catchers to hit with their throws. Add two stopwatches and time the glove-to-glove throws to increase competition between catchers.

Coaching Points

Make sure catchers are using proper technique with their footwork during their throws. Catchers should be aware of their quickness on their hand-to-ball release.

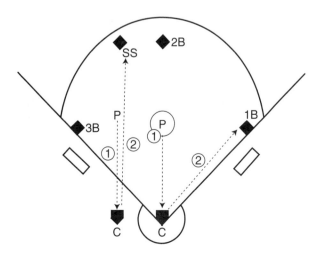

Purpose

To increase the strength and quickness of the catcher's legs in moving from squat to field position

Organization

You'll need a home plate and a bucket of balls. Place a catcher in her normal position behind home plate and place 10 balls around her in fair and foul territory. The balls should be 10 to 15 feet (3 to 4.5 meters) from the catcher and evenly spaced in a circle around her. The catcher should ideally be in full gear to simulate a game situation.

Execution

On command, the catcher jumps up from her squat position and sprints to the first ball and touches it. She then sprints back to her catching position and, once squatted, jumps up and sprints to the next ball in the circle. This shuttle-touch drill continues until all the balls around the circle have been touched. Make sure the catcher sets up in proper position behind home plate.

Variations

This drill can initially be done with fewer than 10 balls if the catcher's strength and endurance are not game ready. Increase the number of balls and reps as the catcher gets stronger. For competition, the drill can be timed to help motivate catchers to be as quick as possible. Change the location of the first ball from in front of home plate to behind home plate. Another timing variation is to give catchers a time limit (such as 30 seconds) and see how many touches they can get before time expires.

Coaching Points

Make sure catchers aren't getting too wide in their ready position. This ensures that they are keeping their weight on the balls of their feet.

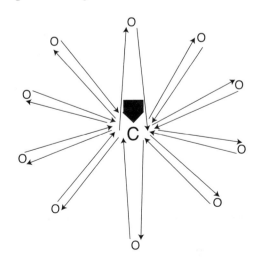

Tactical Drills

Chapter 13

Team Offense

Carol Hutchins University of Michigan Head Coach

The concept of softball is very simple. The team with the most runs at the end of the game wins. A great team is consistently a team of balance in the three statistical categories: pitching, defense, and offense. Because offensive development tends to be the most time consuming of these three basic tenets of softball, it's important to devote a large part of your daily practice to offense. This improves the chance that your players will be equally strong on offense and defense. No matter how natural a hitter may be or may not be, you can make that hitter better. Adjusting the mentality from just being a hitter to playing a "part" in the total offense is in and of itself a challenge to the young player. Strategies are needed when a team is not consistently producing runs, and each member of the lineup should realize her role and understand that she's part of your total offense. Most players will flourish in an environment based on a combination of fundamental skill development, including daily repetition, and instilling a mental approach to hitting that facilitates toughness at the plate.

Success on offense can be thought of in both physical and mental terms. Nearly every daily practice should include a hitting circuit, which is simply drill work and repetition to improve the hitter's swing. As a result of this repetition and drill work, your hitters will *trust* their swings. Trusting your swing allows you to go to the plate focusing on the incoming pitch and not on the mechanics of the physical act of swinging. On mental terms, helping players learn to control their thought processes and to approach each at-bat as a new opportunity for success is important in developing a good hitting team. In softball, every pitch of every at-bat is an opportunity. Regardless of what happened on the last pitch, the last at-bat, or the last game, the *next pitch* is the only pitch your players should focus on. Many hitters allow themselves to be ruled by their emotions, both positive and negative. Those hitters ride a roller coaster of success and tend to be streaky. Athletes who respond emotionally after an at-bat in practice, be it hitting their helmet or tossing their bat, should immediately receive guidance and instruction in trying to identify a more appropriate response to the situation. The only acceptable response after an at-bat is to hustle, either to the base or back to the dugout. When the hitter develops to the point that she sees every pitch as an opportunity, she gives herself the best chance of having a successful at-bat.

Another concept you can incorporate into your approach to offense is that the *process* is more indicative of a good at-bat than is the outcome. In this way you can teach your hitters to recognize when they have had "good at-bats." A definition of having a good at-bat can include hitting hittable pitches, taking nonhittable pitches, fending off two-strike close pitches, and staying in the at-bat for as long as possible. Many a good at-bat can end in a strikeout, just as many a poor at-bat can end with a base hit. Ultimately, the goal is to have your hitters focus on hitting the ball hard rather than on whether their hit counts in the scorebook.

Another aspect of offensive philosophy is the concept of creating an aggressive offense. As a coach, teaching your hitters to be aggressive is the greatest challenge you can face. A good hitting team is an offensively aggressive team that is consistently attacking the pitcher. Your hitters should own the plate. You can use the term "hittable pitches" as opposed to "strikes" when it comes to looking at which pitches you want your batters to swing at. In coaching your hitters to be aggressive, instruct and encourage them to swing at the first hittable pitch. In general, you don't want to be a team that takes a lot of pitches, unless a situation dictates the need to do that. Instilling this philosophy can be extremely difficult. Fear is one of the greatest obstacles a player has in trying to develop into a great hitter. The fear of making a mistake or the fear of failure is often the biggest obstacle for a young hitter. Being able to control their thoughts and to move on to the next pitch is imperative in becoming consistent offensive performers.

Equally important is an aggressive approach on the bases and the ability of the team to use all opportunities when on base to get home. Good base running is an important part of the team offensive attack, and teaching your players not only how to run the bases but how to "read" the ball off the bat is imperative to a good offense. A base runner with a good read on the ball has the best chance to advance, and the best base runners are a step ahead before they ever have to rely on a base coach. Run production is a statistic that should not be overlooked, and learning which hitters can produce with runners in scoring position can ultimately shape your lineup. With run production in mind, try to create those opportunities in the practice setting to develop your offensive approach each year.

Combining an aggressive, mentally tough approach with sound hitting mechanics is a key factor in becoming a good hitting program. As a coach, creating an offensive philosophy that includes fundamentals and mental training along with aggressiveness on the base paths will give your program a guaranteed advantage. These drills will help you get your players to where you want them to be offensively.

149   SIX PITCH

Purpose
To work on selectivity of pitches (hitting strikes and taking balls)

Organization
The batter will be in the batter's box and can get a maximum of six pitches, balls or strikes.

Execution
The batter is to swing at strikes (hittable pitches) and take any nonstrikes or unhittable pitches. If she takes a strike, she's out (done); if she swings at a ball, she's done. The maximum number of pitches in this drill is six, regardless of whether she takes them all or hits them all. The hitter is rewarded if she gets to a total of six points.

Variation
Penalize the hitter for pulling the ball, hitting pop-ups, or any mis-hits.

Coaching Points
In this drill we're teaching our hitters when to swing and when not to. If they happen to take all six, and they are all unhittable pitches, they win the drill. If they swing at all six, and they are all good pitches to hit, they also win the drill. This is an excellent way to practice pitch selection and working the count.

Purpose

To work on short periods of focus during batting practice; to force hitters to make adjustments in a short period of time; to simulate game hitting

Organization

Hitters will be ready to go in groups of three or four at the plate and at the on-deck circle.

Execution

Each hitter gets anywhere from three to six pitches batting-practice style and then hustles to the end of the group. Hitters can go through the drill as many times as the coach requests.

Coaching Points

Hitters must maintain a gamelike approach to their batting practice. They're focused for three to six pitches at a time (just as in a game). No "one more"s allowed.

Purpose

To hit with a purpose in a routine batting practice; to work on moving runners with the short game, by hitting behind the runner in hit and runs, and by scoring the runner from 3B with a sacrifice fly

Organization

Each hitter gets pitches in sets of three. Each set has a specific focus.

Execution

The first set will be a bunt (*a*, runner on 1B), slap (*b*, to right side to move the runner from 2B to 3B), and squeeze (*c*, must bunt the next pitch because the runner is stealing home).

The second set will be a hit and run, followed by a hit on the ground, preferably to the opposite field (runner on 2B advances to 3B), and then a sacrifice fly with a runner on 3B (drive the ball to the outfield).

Coaching Points

Although you can use actual base runners, this drill is typically used with only verbal cues from the coach and can be used in a batting cage, if necessary. This drill gives your hitters some focal points as they simulate actual situations they'll be in during games.

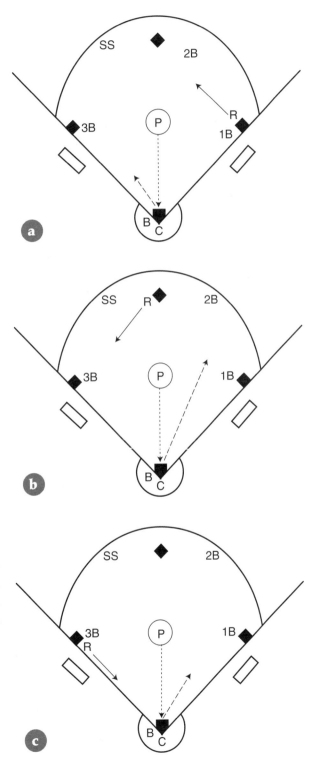

152 POINT GAME

Purpose
To bring some competitive spirit to practice while incorporating run production using both hitting and base running in a competitive drill; to work on getting to base and advancing base runners

Organization
Divide your offense into equal groups. Put a full defensive team on the field. The pitcher can be the batting practice pitcher or your competitive pitcher, depending on how difficult and realistic you want the game to be.

Execution
Each team bats (don't call balls and strikes), and although the defense will either get an out or give up a base (points), bat through the entire lineup before changing offensive teams. A team will hit, get to base, and stay on the base—or get all the way home—unless they are forced out by the defense or the defense gets to three outs. At three outs, the bases are cleared, and the offense can resume if they have not made it through the lineup.

Points are awarded per base:

1B = 1 point

2B = 2 points

3B = 3 points

Home = 4 points

For every base that a team member touches safely, her team receives a point each (e.g., a double would be 1 point + 2 points for a total of 3. A home run would be a total of all the bases, or 1 + 2 + 3 + 4 = 10 points. Each team is competing against all other teams, so the team at the end of the game with the most points wins.

Coaching Points
Emphasize getting to base and advancing base runners. This drill breaks the offensive game into smaller pieces. A team can outscore opponents without ever touching home plate.

153   CONSEQUENCES

Purpose

To create situations in practice that put a perceived pressure on player performance and outcome; to practice playing under gamelike pressure

Organization

Create any situation desired (executing a bunt, a hit and run, a squeeze, and so on). The drill can include both the hitting and base-running component of the strategy. Any lack of execution of the drill (e.g., the hitter pops up or the base runner loses track of the ball) results in a consequence that's imparted on the offending player(s). Just as in a game, lack of execution has a consequence: either making an out or losing a game. In this drill, lack of execution has a consequence as well (running extra sprints, doing push-ups, singing for the rest of the team).

Variation

Allow a chance at times for "double or nothing" in which players can choose to redo a skill that they have not executed properly; if they don't execute successfully the second time, their penalty is double, such as twice the number of sprints. This creates an atmosphere of players "going for it." I like to reward this behavior because it's a quality I most want in my team. I like to see my players have no fear of the possibility of failure.

Coaching Points

Remind your team not to focus on the consequence but on executing the objective properly. The consequence essentially serves as a potential distraction to the player, and it's her job to overcome it.

Purpose

To practice short-game offensive situations in a practice setting, creating opportunities for repetition for hitters and base runners

Organization

Place a hitter in the batter's box and a base runner at the base at which the situation will occur. You may use a full defense or simply drill offensively without a defense.

Execution

Offensive players in the drill line up at the plate; one hitter comes up at a time. Base runners form their line near their respective base. Hitters are given one pitch to execute the offense.

Variations

The following are the many short-game situations that occur during the course of a game:

Sacrifice bunt with runner at 1B: The hitter squares as the pitcher begins her motion. The runner releases from base using a three-step lead and keeps her feet in motion toward 2B. The object is to get to 2B safely.

Bunt and run: The runner steals 2B; the hitter *must* get the next pitch bunted safely. Tell runners to go from 1B to 3B in this drill as they should learn to look to advance all the way to 3B on this play.

Sacrifice bunt with runner on 2B: The hitter squares on the pitcher's motion and bunts a buntable pitch (i.e., a strike). The runner takes a big lead (five steps); although she isn't stealing 3B, she's advancing very aggressively.

Safety bunt with runner on 3B: The hitter squares on the pitcher's motion; the runner takes her leadoff only as far as the third baseman allows. (Don't go past the third baseman.) If the ball is bunted, the runner advances on release of the ball from the fielder as she throws to 1B. (The runner is not required to advance.)

Squeeze bunt with runner at 3B: The runner is stealing the base (home) and leaves aggressively on release of the pitch. The hitter squares *late* and must bunt (or at least make contact with) the next pitch to protect the runner. (Even a foul ball protects the runner.)

Coaching Points

It's important to discuss the roles of each player and the ultimate goal for the different types of short-game situations. Athletes will be more motivated and execute at a higher success level if they understand how the different types of short game work together in establishing offensive strategy. Make sure that the athletes know ideal placement and strengths for the different types of bunts executed.

Purpose

To drill the various offensive situations that put runners in motion on the pitch

Organization

Runners begin at a base; a hitter takes position in the batter's box, ready to execute her part of the offensive strategy.

Execution

Hitters get *one pitch* to execute the motion offense. Runners are stealing on the pitch and must know where the ball is at all times!

Variations

Hit and run: The runner steals the base (either 2B or 3B), taking a look to find the ball on her third step. The hitter *must* hit the next pitch. Teach hitters to put the ball on the ground and, preferably, behind the runner. You can run this play with a runner on 1B or 2B.

Run and hit: The runner tries to steal the base (takes a look to find the ball on third step); the hitter swings at strikes only (hittable pitches). The hitter is not mandated to hit the ball.

Fake hit and run: The runner steals the base; the hitter swings and intentionally misses the next pitch. (The hitter needs to sell the swing as a real attempt to hit the ball!)

Fake bunt and steal: The runner tries to steal the base; the hitter shows a bunt (squares late) to protect the runner and freeze the defense.

Contact play: A runner is on 3B. The hitter tries to put the ball in play; she might choke up and attempt just to put the ball on the ground. The runner is breaking for home on contact *regardless* of where the ball is hit.

Angle down: A runner is on 3B. The hitter is trying to put the ball on the ground toward the second baseman or the SS. The runner breaks for home if the ball is hit through the first line of defense (pitcher, first baseman, or third baseman).

Coaching Points

Solid communication when athletes fail is important. Since they only get one attempt to execute, there will be much failure in the beginning. Give the athlete a full understanding of the expectations and role of each player. One approach to this drill is to create holes in the defense, and then the batter must take advantage of those defensive holes.

Purpose

To require athletes to execute a successful bunt while creating gamelike pressure

Organization

Hitters (bunters) line up at the plate; an equal number of runners line up at 1B.

Execution

The coach allots a set time (under two minutes) for the team to consecutively bunt the runners at 1B to 2B. For instance, if you have 14 bunters, you're looking for 14 consecutive successful bunts in under two minutes to complete the drill. Base runners practice reading the bunt off the bat and releasing to 2B.

Variations

Decrease the time allotted; squeeze with the runner on 3B.

Coaching Points

Anytime you add pressure you will create more gamelike intensity. Your athletes will feel real and perceived peer pressure to succeed for their team. If there is consistent failure by a single player, it will help you to find out if the pressure and not the skill is what is causing her to fail more often.

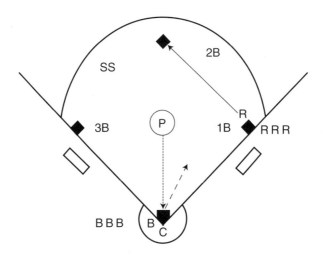

ISOLATION OFFENSE

Purpose

To help base runners read the ball off the bat and learn to anticipate the ball as contact is made; to teach your athletes what is expected at each base in order to maximize their success

Organization

During a routine batting practice a base runner occupies each base and reacts to each ball hit as if she's the only runner on base. Establish the expectations at each base so the athlete can specifically react or execute the offensive situation at each base.

Execution

Bases only appear to be loaded in that each runner is isolated and working on her own base running from her own base. Coaches should create a list of potential scenarios that the runners will need to judge or react to at each base. For example, the first round, have the runners on first working on a straight steal with the hitter being live. The first-base runner will need to sneak a peak and react as the ball is hit. The runner on second could be working on an aggressive read for a tie game situation late in the game. The runner on third could have an aggressive angle read situation. Be specific so all the runners will know their roles and what they are working on.

Coaching Points

Revolve base runners around the bases so they can practice reading and reacting from 1B, 2B, and 3B to different situations. Keep the athletes working from the same base for an entire batter. When you switch hitters, you can advance the runners one base, and they will work on the established scenario for that base. You can have multiple runners at one base so they can work easily without needing to rush back to the base before the next pitch. This will allow for batting practice to continue at an appropriate rate, and you will not need to wait for the runners to return to the base. Also it is important that hitters return as quickly as they can to maximize their reps at each base, but they should only attempt to execute the scenario if they are able to make it back to the base in time to make it gamelike.

Purpose
To create a situation in which the runner is in scoring position and the hitter's goal is to get an RBI

Organization
A runner is on 2B. A hitter is at the plate. This drill can be done with a full defense on the field, or it can be done with an imaginary defense with the hitter reacting accordingly.

Execution
Batters take a gamelike at-bat with balls and strikes called. Hitters attempt to hit the ball and score the runner. A point is awarded to each batter if she scores. Keep a tally for all hitters participating in the drill.

Coaching Points
Adding a competition-like intensity to the situation helps to expose athletes' weaknesses under pressure. Use these types of drills to get a better understanding of the mental approach of your athletes when runners are in scoring position.

Purpose

To create a competitive environment in which a team maximizes its offensive production

Organization

Place all offensive players in one dugout. They should organize their own batting order based on maximizing offensive production. On the defensive side, use all nonoffensive players, pitchers who don't hit, coaches, managers, trainers, and anyone willing to play on defense. The defense may have more than nine players. The defense players may play in any positions on the field and are not limited to normal defensive alignments. If you have a batting practice pitcher, she can throw to the offensive players. If not, use a pitching machine.

Execution

Each offensive player steps to the plate for her at-bat. Players can not walk or strike out. They may choose to bunt, slap, or hit to get on base. Each batter runs out her hit; if she's safe, she stays on base. If the defense makes the out, the defense scores a point. The offense can score points only when a runner crosses the plate. The object is for the offense to score 21 points, or runs, before the defense gets 21 outs. Runners aren't allowed to steal but can be running on the pitch. They can only advance when the batter puts the ball in play.

Variations

Set a time limit on the game. Give batters a set number of pitches to put a ball into play or else her at-bat is ruled an out. If using pitching machines, place two machines side by side and simulate an off-speed pitch or change-up from one machine.

Coaching Points

Offensive players are encouraged to use all their offensive skills (aside from stealing) to advance the runners. The competitive spirit to compete against the coaches can create an enjoyable and extremely motivated game.

Purpose

To stress the importance of using all aspects of team offensive skills

Organization

Divide your team into two or more equal groups. Ideally, you want enough players to field a full defense while the other group is batting. If you have 12 players, use 3 teams of 4 players. Place one team on offense and the other two teams on defense. Place a pitching machine on the mound with a protective net for the feeder.

Make up a scorecard for your teams to use. This scorecard should include the potential offensive skill or strategies you want your team to work on (see sample). Coaches should evenly divide team leaders and star players onto separate teams.

	First attempt		Second attempt		Third attempt		Bonus points for three executions	
Home run	5 pts		5 pts		5 pts		50 pts	
RBI single	3 pts		3 pts		3 pts		25 pts	
Sac bunt	3 pts		3 pts		3 pts		20 pts	
Slap bunt	2 pts		2 pts		2 pts		15 pts	
Squeeze	5 pts		5 pts		5 pts		50 pts	
Hit and run	3 pts		3 pts		3 pts		25 pts	
Sac fly	2 pts		2 pts		2 pts		15 pts	
Bonus points for execution of full set	50 pts		50 pts		50 pts			
Sub totals								
Total								

Execution

Each team gets 21 attempts to execute, which simulates the 21 outs in a seven-inning game. The offense must bat all players in a set order but can choose which offensive strategy each batter will attempt. For every failure to execute on an attempt, the offense must cross off or eliminate one of the 21 attempts on their scorecard; the box eliminated does not have to match the strategy that failed. This strategy feature allows players to maximize their own team's strengths and minimize categories that their team is not good at (e.g., if their team doesn't have power hitters they can eliminate the home run boxes). Notice that a team can gain high bonus points for three successful executions or for filling out a full sequence of execution attempts. The defense takes a gamelike approach and attempts to keep the offensive team from succeeding.

Variations

To make the challenge more difficult, require that each player on a team can be used only once per skill, which means three different players must successfully execute each skill. If you want to stress a particular aspect of team offense, add or delete skills or change the values for successful executions (e.g., if your team struggles with bunting, give a successful bunt attempt a higher value).

Coaching Points

Ideally, your leaders or captains will learn how to organize their team's strategy to maximize their team's ability to score points. Before you begin, you might want to give the offensive teams five minutes to figure out which players will execute which skills. Team leaders should be encouraged to maximize their team's strengths and avoid random strategies.

Purpose

To give batters and base runners many repetitions at reading the ball off the bat while working on short-game skills

Organization

Divide your team into four equal groups. All runners should have helmets on. There should be a group at each base and one group at home to be batters. You can do this drill with a live batting practice pitcher (ideally) or with a pitching machine.

Execution

Designate what the runner's responsibility will be at each base, as well as what skill the batter is to work on (e.g., begin the drill by working on sacrifice bunts). The runners on first should be working on their leads and reading and reacting to the bunt (advancing on good bunts, returning on pop-ups, and so on). The runners at 2B should work on a straight steal on the pitcher's release (or machine delivery) and sneaking a peek toward home to see if the ball is popped up. Runners on 3B should work on aggressively reacting to the ball's angle off the bat. They should break for home on any ball that comes off the bat and heads downward. They don't need to read fair or foul, just the ball's angle off the bat, and should try to get an aggressive jump. Runners advance to the next base and go to the back of the line at each base or at home plate to await their turn as batter. Once the entire team has had a turn, the coach can change the expectation of the batter or the responsibilities at each base.

Coaching Points

All runners should sprint through the next base when appropriate. They need to keep their actions between bases as gamelike as possible, with no jogging, trotting, or easy running. When altering the responsibilities or expectations, be creative and make sure that any skill you'll need in a game is incorporated. As always, make sure players are working with gamelike intensity and being as realistic as possible. Most important, clearly define what you expect the runners to do at each base before beginning.

Purpose

To teach batters when, where, and how to use the hit and run with runners in different positions on the base paths

Organization

You'll need a pitching machine in front of the pitching mound on a regulation field. Split your team into two or more groups. Use more than two if you have a large team and would like to have one team on defense shagging balls. One team will work as batters, and the other team will work as runners.

Execution

Start with all runners at 1B, with one player running at a time. Give each batter one attempt to execute a hit and run with the runner at 1B. Runners will advance to 2B and wait for all of the players at 1B to complete their turn at 1B. Once all hitters have been given their rep with runners on 1B, they are then given their rep at a hit and run with a runner on 2B. As each runner advances to 3B, she will wait until all runners from 2B have advanced to 3B. Once all runners are at 3B, batters will get a rep at attempting to score the runner on 3B with a hit-and-run play.

Coaching Points

Be sure to explain to batters and runners where the gaps in the defense will probably open up when the runner is stealing on the pitch. Have batters focus on hitting to the open areas. Many coaches have their players choke up on the bat and almost pepper the ball.

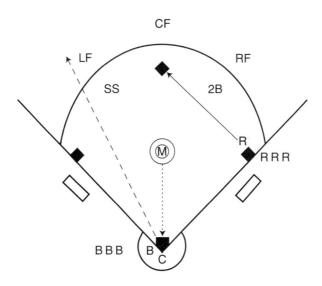

Purpose

To work on executing offensive strategy; to train base runners on proper reaction

Organization

Divide your team into groups of four to five players. All offensive players should wear helmets. Place a runner at each base on a regulation field. A batter comes up to the plate, and another is on deck. Use either a batting practice pitcher or a pitching machine, depending on the level of difficulty you want to create.

Execution

The batter will take three consecutive attempts to successfully execute three different offensive strategies under gamelike pressure. The first attempt *(a)* will be with a runner on 3B. The runner will advance home on the play and prepare to be the next batter on deck. The second attempt *(b)* will be with a runner on 2B. This runner will advance on the attempt and stay at 3B for the next batter. The third attempt *(c)* will be with a runner on 1B only. This runner will also advance on the play to the next base and be in place for the next batter. On this third and final attempt, the batter will run through 1B and become the 1B runner for the next batter.

The new batter steps to the plate and executes the same three offensive strategies. All batters in this group get three attempts at the plate as well as work on the base paths as runners.

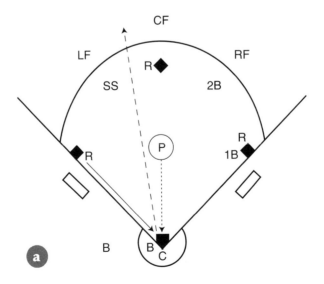

Coaching Points

The coach determines which three offensive strategies will be worked on each round. With the runner at 3B you could work on squeeze plays, safety squeezes, hit and runs, tagging up, or aggressive ball angle reads. With the runner on 1B or 2B you could work on sac bunts, slap bunts, push bunts, straight steals with batter protection, or hitting behind the runner. The coach should give a specific situation at each base for the three attempts.

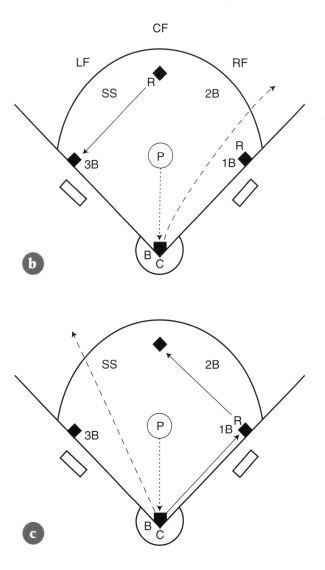

Purpose

To practice the many different ways to work the first-and-third situation on offense

Organization

Defensive players and a pitcher set up on a regulation infield. Remaining players are base runners (with helmets) at 1B and 3B. You also need a batter at home.

Execution

Players practice running a variety of offensive plays for the first-and-third play. As each player takes her turn at a base or at home, she will advance to the next position to make sure that all players practice and experience the offensive strategy from the base runners' positions and the batter's box.

Coaching Points

Clearly define each player's roles for each of the plays she'll be expected to run. If the batter has a role, she too should be executing the play as you expect. Rotate your infielders, pitchers, and catchers into the base runner rotation so they can practice too. It's fine to place outfielders at infield positions for this drill.

Chapter 14

Team Defense

Yvette Girouard Louisiana State University Head Coach

The past decade has witnessed the technological advancement of the offensive component of our great game of fastpitch softball. Bat technology, the physical development of players, and diversity of offensive strategies have steered the game toward more offensive production. However, despite the offensive explosion of our sport, the age-old foundations of team defense remain unchanged. These basic principles of defense still hold true:

1. If your opponent never touches home plate, your team cannot lose.
2. The team that makes the fewest number of fielding and throwing errors usually wins the game.
3. A defender should charge the ball whenever possible.
4. You should always assume the ball is coming to you, and you must know what you're going to do with it when you get it.
5. Defense must be played with passion; you must "want the ball."

The ability to perform the basic skills of throwing, catching, fielding, and communicating is the determining factor in team success. These skills come into play from the most routine to the most elite game strategies. Incorporating these fundamental skills of the game into situational strategies is the next step in the development of your team's defensive concept. When advancing to these situational strategies, the bottom line is to keep things simple. Repetition of the basic skills and strategies through drills and practice should build confidence in your players that carries over to their performance in games. Once they understand the basics of the strategies at play, they should always perform their drills at game speed to maximize the team's defensive efficiency and execution. The drills in this chapter accentuate the concept of team defense and make the skills trained in practice more gamelike.

Communication, both verbal and nonverbal, is the beginning and ending link to the success of team defense. Unfortunately, time spent on team defensive communication often takes a back seat to physical skill training. But you should never underestimate the importance of effective communication in team defense. Make time in every practice for drills that focus on verbal communication among defensive positions. Defensive play-making priorities must be discussed and established. The centerfielder commonly has priority over the other outfielders, meaning that if she calls for the ball, she is to make the play while the other outfielders back her up. The entire outfield has priority over the infield: If an outfielder and an infielder are making a play on the ball and are both calling for it, the infielder should yield to the outfielder. Among the infield, the middle infielders usually have priority over the corners and the pitcher, whereas the corners usually have priority over the catcher in making calls on the ball. Although these are not steadfast rules of team defense, the understanding and practicing of these concepts in some shape or form is crucial to the effective and safe execution of team defense and should never be overlooked. Several of the drills that follow highlight the concepts of team defensive communication that require diligent work in practice if your players are to be fully prepared for situations that occur during games.

165   21 IN A ROW

Purpose
To emphasize that in the game of fastpitch softball, 21 outs must be properly executed to complete seven innings of defensive play

Organization
Use a standard field setup with a player at each defensive position. A coach is needed to hit the ball into play; runners are placed at home plate to run for the hitter.

Execution
The defense begins with no outs and must make 21 outs in a row without committing an error. If an error is committed, the out count returns to zero. After a ball is hit into play by the coach, the runners from home plate become base runners. If a ball is hit safely, the runners stay on base to create situations. Once three outs are made, the bases are cleared. The drill is not complete until the 21st out is recorded.

Variations
Defensive and base-running substitutions can be made at any time. The coach may fungo the ball into play for better control or hit off of a tee for a different read for the defense. The coach can hit the ball as randomly as desired or as methodically as desired to set up situations. Bonus outs may be awarded for outstanding plays in the field (e.g., diving or sliding catches).

Coaching Points
This can be a challenging defensive drill that incorporates a myriad of situations. The coach putting the ball into play has the control to set up practically any defensive situation and to test it at will. This drill can also test the fight, determination, and will of the defense in adverse conditions. Depending on the difficulty of the balls put into play, this drill can be very time consuming and challenging or can provide a defense with instant confidence. All players feel a sense of achievement after reaching the goal of recording 21 straight outs.

Purpose
To better understand and execute defensive options when defending situations with runners at 1B and 3B

Organization
All infielders take their normal positions.

Execution
After the pitch is delivered, the SS breaks to cover 2B, and the second baseman breaks to her "cut" position, about six feet (two meters) in front and just off line of 2B. In a live first-and-third situation, the defense must react to runners at 1B and 3B, but in this drill there are no base runners. Infielders should practice each of the six basic ways to defend this situation:

A: Throw down to 2B; SS lays the tag at 2B.

B: Throw down to 2B; SS cuts the ball at 2B and throws the ball directly home to prevent the runner at 3B from scoring.

C: Throw down to 2B; second baseman cuts the ball and throws to 3B to tag the runner who is too far off the bag.

D: Throw down to 2B; second baseman cuts the ball and throws directly to home to prevent the runner at 3B from scoring.

E: Throw down to 2B; second baseman cuts the ball and flips the ball to SS. SS walks the runner back to 1B while checking the runner at 3B.

F: Throw down to 3B; third baseman tags the runner who's too far off the bag.

Variation
Once the options are understood and worked through smoothly, use outfielders as live base runners so that the defense can react to their leads, breaks, and positioning on the base paths.

Coaching Points
When cutting the throw down to 2B, it's important to meet the ball and catch the throw on the right foot (for right-handed players). This enables the defender to throw on the very next (left) step. The second baseman should always cut the throw down to 2B if the throw is too high or off line.

The runner on 3B is the priority out in first-and-third situations, because this runner holds the threat of scoring. If this runner breaks to home at any point during a first-and-third situation, the defender should remove her focus from the runner at 1B and turn it fully to the runner at 3B to prevent her from scoring.

It's helpful to use the coach's box as a reference point when determining if the runner on 3B is too far off the base. If the runner is past the coach's box, a throw can be made to 3B. If the runner is halfway between 3B and home, force her to commit back to 3B or on to home by running directly at her (a rundown situation).

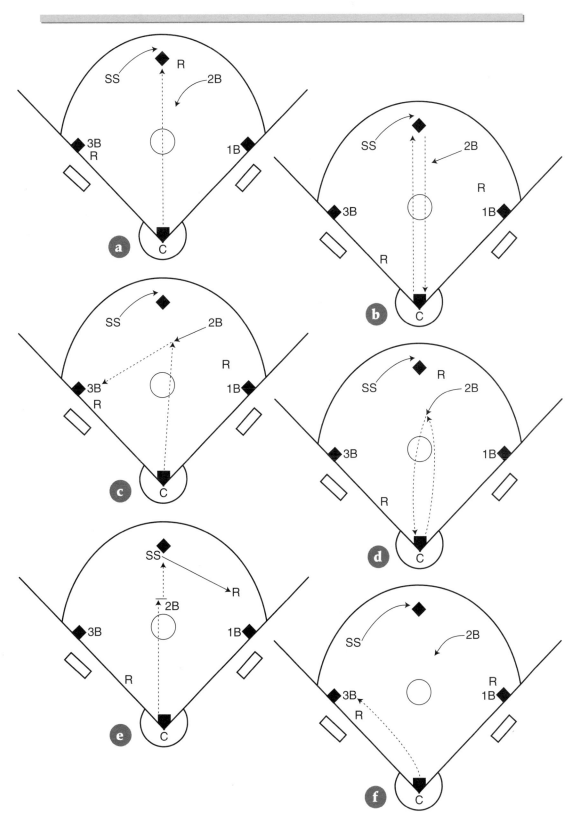

Purpose

To systematically get balls hit to each position, working both the infield and the outfield

Organization

Use a standard field setup, with all players taking a specified number of reps at their positions. One coach hits fungos from home plate. One extra infielder or pitcher stands off to the side of the catcher and receives balls thrown in from the third baseman. This extra player feeds balls to the catcher who in turn feeds the coach.

Execution

The coach begins the round of fungo by hitting one fly ball to the left fielder. The left fielder hits her cut (SS), who then fires the ball to the second baseman covering 2B. After the second baseman lays the tag at 2B, she throws the ball to the third baseman covering 3B. After the third baseman lays the tag at 3B, she fires the ball home to the extra player at home plate. The coach then rotates the fungo to the centerfield and right-field positions, with those successive throws in from the outfield making the rounds at 2B and 3B. After each outfielder gets a fly ball going into 2B, the coach rotates the fungo around the outfield, with

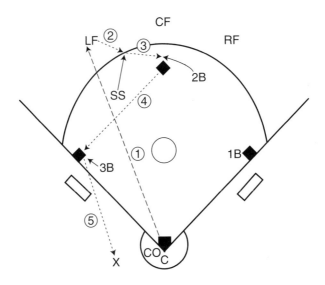

throws coming into 3B. The last round of balls hit to the outfield come into home plate, with the catcher making the tag. Once the outfielders have completed their rounds, the catcher begins the infield rounds with throws to the infielders at their positions, beginning with the third baseman and followed by the SS, second baseman, and first baseman. The drill should be rapid fire. If more than one catcher is available, each one can begin a round of throws to the infield. After the catcher's throws are complete, the coach then begins to hit grounders to the infield, beginning with the third baseman, who makes the play at 1B. Once the play at 1B is made, the first baseman throws the ball to 3B, where the third baseman covers the bag and makes the tag. Once the tag at 3B is complete, the ball is thrown in to the extra player who's feeding the catcher. The coach then makes the rounds to the other infielders (SS, second baseman, first baseman, pitcher, and catcher).

Variations

The coach can dictate how many balls and what types (ground balls, line drives, fly balls) each player gets per round. The coach can choose to add double plays and tag plays at specified bases for each of the infield positions. The coach might also want each player's last ball to be a "one and follow" ball (the player immediately follows her initial play with another ball).

Purpose

To increase repetitions and keep each player moving as fielders make plays at every base

Organization

Use a standard infield setup with a defender at each position, excluding the pitcher. Two coaches are needed to hit ground balls from either side of the batter's boxes. A catcher is needed for each coach. A number is assigned to each position on the field: pitcher (1), catcher (2), first baseman (3), second baseman (4), third baseman (5), and SS (6).

Execution

This drill is divided into four rounds. Hit 10 to 12 balls per round before advancing to the next round. In each round, coaches 1 and 2 hit ground balls to the two infield positions. For rounds 1 through 4, list the infield positions being targeted for each round. The positional players are to make the force or tag play at the position shared in the round. The four rounds are as follows:

Round 1: 5-6, 6-5 / 4-3, 3-4 ("tweeners")
Round 2: 4-6, 6-4 / 5-3, 3-5
Round 3: 6-3, 3-6 / 4-5, 5-4
Round 4: Double plays

Variations

Round 1 ground balls can be hit randomly between the two positions (third baseman and SS, second baseman and first baseman) so that defenders communicate as they field. A special round can be created to include the catcher (2-5, 5-2 / 2-3, 3-2). This provides a chance for the SS and second baseman to catch their breaths.

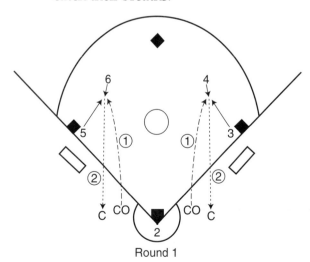

Round 1

Coaching Points

Infielders should be light on the balls of their feet, charging the ball whenever possible. Middle infielders should use j-cuts and angles on balls hit to their left and right. Receivers must show a target on their throwing shoulder. After receiving the ball, players allow one step and then throw the ball in to the coach's assigned catcher. This drill requires concentration because two balls are being hit simultaneously.

Purpose

To work on player communication during high pop-up or shallow fly-ball situations

Organization

The field will be split in half, down the middle from centerfield all the way to the catcher. Players assume their normal fielding positions. The right side of the defense works together, and the left side of the defense does the same. One coach stands in the left-handed batter's box, and another coach is in the right.

Execution

From the batter's boxes, coaches throw high pop-ups and shallow fly balls to the side of the field they're assigned to. Players work together as a unit, focusing on using good communication to field the ball.

Variations

You can use two centerfielders at once, as well as two pitchers and catchers, just as long as each one knows which side of the field she's working with. Once all players complete the desired number of pop-ups and shallow fly balls with the split field, the defense can come together and do the drill as a unit, with one coach throwing from home plate. If the coach is skilled enough, she might want to actually hit fungos for the fly balls and pop-ups to add to the difficulty of the drill. Balls thrown directly against the wind and directly into the line of the sun are especially challenging.

Coaching Points

When possible, run this drill on bright and sunny days with strong winds. This will challenge the defense to communicate and stay with the play until it's complete. On windy days, stress that the part of the field where the ball begins to come down might not be where it actually lands. All positions must be ready to make the play if weather conditions are severe.

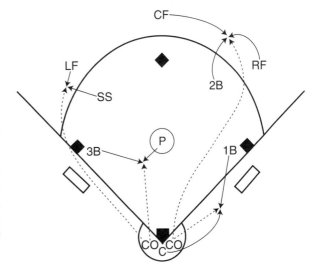

Purpose

To work on player placement and quickness when defending slap hitters and bunters

Organization

Players take their positions on a standard infield setup. Place a tee with a ball on home plate. Outfielders serve as the slap hitters and bunters.

Execution

After the pitcher goes through her pitching motion, the outfielder will hit the ball off of the tee, simulating the style and touch of a slap hitter, and run her hit out. The defense fields the ball and makes the play at 1B. Proceed to creating force-play situations at 2B, 3B, and home plate.

Variations

Keep the defense on their toes by laying down bunts in the midst of the slap hits. Use slap hitters in the lineup to slap hit a live pitch. This makes it possible for the defense to read the ball off a live bat.

Coaching Points

The setup for slap defense should resemble a shrunken infield. The corners must be ready to field the bunt at any point. Depending on the strength of her arm, the SS should be placed just behind or on the baseline. If the slap hitter is extremely quick, it's recommended that the SS play in front of the baseline.

Communication is key when fielding slap hits and bunts. Corners need to keep their shoulders low, side to side, cutting straight to the pitcher's mound. Middle infielders must charge every hit and work a quick release.

Purpose

To secure an out in a defensive situation in which a runner is caught between two bases

Organization

Divide your team into three equal groups (1, 2, and 3). The rundown will occur between 1B and 2B. Group 1 starts at 1B, group 2 starts at 2B, and group 3 runs the bases. One player from groups 1 and 2 assumes the role of the defensive player (DP1 and DP2). One runner from group 3 assumes the role of the base runner (R). The coach tosses the ball to DP1 or DP2 to initiate the rundown.

Execution

DP1 runs toward R, carrying the ball above her throwing shoulder in a dart-like tossing position. She should establish a throwing lane with her receiver, DP2. DP1 makes an effort to tag R; if she does, the drill stops and DP1, DP2, and R go to the end of the line after rotating to the next group. The next players in line then step forward. If DP1 makes an effort to tag R but cannot, she should then make a dart-like throw to DP2. DP1 follows her throw and moves to the back of the line at 2B. Players continue this rotation, following their throws and moving to the end of the receiving line until R has been tagged out. The fewer the throws, the better.

The drill resumes with the coach's toss. Once all base runners have had a turn running, groups rotate, each taking a new role. Group 1 players become base runners. Group 2 players move to 1B. Group 3 players become defensive players at 2B. Groups rotate until all players have had the chance to be base runners.

Coaching Points

When receiving the ball in a rundown, the defensive player should step to the ball as she catches. This closes the distance between herself and the runner and makes it easier to run the runner down. Have base runners wear helmets for safety. When first working on rundowns, use softie balls until the defensive players and base runners can do the drill with confidence; then move to a real ball. It's important that the defensive player stay under control while running toward the base runner, but she must move at good speed to make the runner commit in a retreating direction. All tags should be done with two hands to ensure that the ball doesn't pop out of the glove.

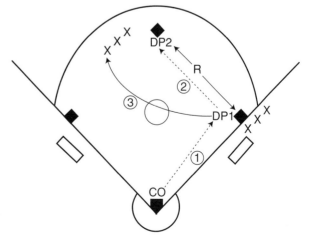

Purpose

To work on player communication and positioning when balls are hit deep into the outfield gaps

Organization

Players take their positions on a standard field. A coach is needed to hit balls deep into the outfield gaps. Begin with one live base runner on 1B, 2B, or 3B, depending on the situation you want to create. A live base runner is also needed at home plate, running for the hitter.

Execution

To begin this drill, the pitcher (on the pitcher's mound) uses her windup motion to simulate the pitch. The coach hits the ball into the left-center deep gap, right-center deep gap, or deep down either base line from home plate. After the ball is hit, a runner from home plate heads to 1B, and all other runners advance. When the ball is hit down the 3B line, the left fielder (LF) should make a play on the ball and then throw the ball into the SS as the first cutoff. When the ball is hit into the left-center gap, the LF and CF should both attempt a play on the ball. Whichever player gets to the ball first should make the play and then throw the ball in to the SS as the first cutoff in the relay. When the ball is hit into the right-center gap, the CF and RF should both attempt a play on the ball. Once again, whichever player gets to the ball first should make the play and throw the ball in to the second baseman going out to assist in the relay.

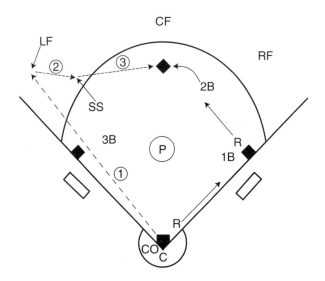

After the first cutoff receives the ball, the catcher should call out where the ball should be thrown to or if it should just be held (if there's no other play). The pitcher watches the base runners and backs up where the play is to be made, in case of an overthrow. The first baseman can be used as the secondary cutoff, positioned to the left or right, standing about halfway between the first relay player and the catcher.

Variations

Variations of this drill will depend on the depth of the ball hit into the gaps and the placement of the base runners. To decrease difficulty, simply hit balls more shallow with runners at 1B or 2B. To increase difficulty, hit balls deeper into the gaps with runners at 3B or 2B.

Coaching Points

Outfielders should take proper angles and use good communication in relation to back-up responsibilities. Infielders position to properly cover bases that base runners might advance to, while ensuring that all cutoff responsibility is properly covered as well. The catcher must be extra alert during this drill, recognizing the speed of the runners on the bases, as well as the speed of the hitter to make a good judgment call to the infielders for a proper cutoff call. Check for proper positioning of all players, and then focus on good communication. The catcher must let the play develop fully and make a good judgment call for a proper cutoff. This is not easy and will take lots of practice.

Purpose

To work on defensive preparation for an upcoming competition by informing the team of the opponent's lineup and player tendencies

Organization

Players take their positions on a standard field. A coach is needed to hit balls to the defense. A scouting report is needed on the opposing team.

Execution

The scouting report should provide information on the order of the lineup and each player's offensive tendencies. The coach acts as each of the nine hitters in the opponent's lineup. For example, if the leadoff batter is a left-handed slap hitter, the defense will set up in slap defense arrangement, and the coach will slap from the left side of the plate. The coach takes the defense through all nine hitters in the opposing team's lineup.

Variations

After completion of the nine batters, practice team offense by challenging the offense to score a certain number of runs off of the opponent's pitcher. Give the scouting report on the pitcher (her pitches, placement, go-to pitch, and speed). A coach or pitcher can represent the opposing pitcher by replicating her pitching tendencies. Continue for a number of innings, alternating playing defense and offense versus the future opponent.

Coaching Points

This drill provides a great deal of preparation for the team's upcoming competition against a team that has been scouted well.

Purpose

To work on proper team defensive techniques in gamelike pressure situations

Organization

Players take their positions on a standard field. A coach is needed to hit balls into play from home plate. A base runner is placed at 3B at the beginning of every play. Runners are also needed to run from home plate to simulate the hitter advancing.

Execution

The defense is placed in a situation in which a runner is always beginning at 3B with fewer than two outs. The defense is instructed to make sure that the runner doesn't score while making the proper play to get the batter out. The coach hits the ball once to each position in a random order. After each player has made a successful play, the drill is over.

Variations

The coach can inform the defense that each player has to make a set number of plays, thereby making the successive rounds more random. The coach can have signals with the base runners from 3B (e.g., suicide squeeze, advance home on any ground ball, delayed steal, first-and-third opportunities, etc.) to make the rounds more challenging.

Coaching Points

The coach must have a good read of the defensive mindset of the team during this drill. The coach can also direct the infield to come in, stay back, warn of potential trick offensive plays, and direct any outfield assist opportunities. Use this drill to test a defense's ability to keep balls in the infield and challenge the outfield's throws on any given play.

Purpose

To work on player communication and placement when throwing balls in from the outfield

Organization

Players take their positions on a standard field. A coach is needed to hit balls to the outfielders. Begin with one live base runner on 1B, 2B, or 3B, depending on the situation you would like to create. A live base runner is also needed at home plate to run for the hitter.

Execution

After the coach hits the ball to an outfielder and the base runner advances, the outfielder must field the ball and throw it in to the infield as efficiently as possible. The infielders cover a base or line up the throw to the next base that the runner will advance to. A rule of thumb is to line up the throw two bases ahead of where the base runner begins (e.g., if the runner begins on 1B, the throw will be lined up to 3B). The infielder must listen for the catcher to direct whether the ball should be cut off. The infielder must relay the throw if the ball is off line or if the ball is dying.

The pitcher must back up 3B or home. The catcher has view of the entire field and must communicate where to throw the ball. Keep communication from the catcher clear and simple: Call out, "Three!" multiple times if the throw should be lined up to 3B. If there's no play because the runner did not advance or already beat the throw, call out, "Cut!" multiple times. If there's another play after the ball has been cut, call out, "Cut two (or one)!" multiple times. Never call out, "Cut hold," because it sounds like "Cut home." Depending on where the ball is hit and where the base runners are located, many options can develop within this drill.

Ball hit to RF with runner on 1B.

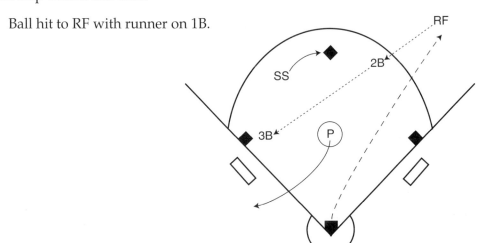

Ball hit to RF with runner on 2B.

Ball hit to CF with runner on 1B.

Ball hit to CF with runner on 2B.

(continued)

Ball hit to LF with runner on 1B.

Ball hit to LF with runner on 2B.

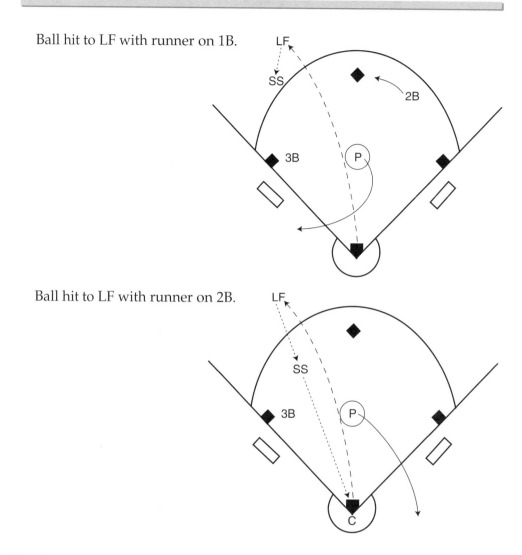

Variations

Prior to using base runners and hitting balls to the outfield, walk through each situation and placement of defenders. Following a walk-through, hit balls to the outfielders without the presence of base runners.

Coaching Points

Every defender has responsibilities when running relays and cutoffs. If the defender is not directly involved in the play, she'll need to cover an empty base or back up a throw. The key to running relays and cutoffs smoothly is clear communication among defenders. The catcher must be the most vocal, because she has full sight of the field and base runners in view. Footwork is crucial when relaying a throw. Meet and catch the ball on the right foot, followed by the one step and throw.

Purpose
To work on perfecting communication among infielders and outfielders

Organization
Break the team up into four groups of players: two infield groups and two outfield groups. Place one infield group at the SS position and the other at 2B. There should be an outfield group directly behind the infield group in the RCF gap and LCF gap areas. These players should create four points. The left-side groups work together, and the right-side groups work together. If you have players that play both infield and outfield, they can switch positions after each of their repetitions. Players should switch infield and outfield lines to make sure they are working with different players. Finally, you'll need a coach with a bucket of balls standing at the pitcher's mound.

Execution
The coach alternates throwing pop flys to the left side and right side of the field. It's important that the coach lets players know what they should be calling and when. There are many different styles or ways to communicate, but most important is that all of your team knows the expectations for infielders and outfielders. The ball needs to be called by the peak of its flight to prevent collisions.

Coaching Points
Players need a clear understanding of the expectations before beginning the drill. The coach can start by tossing the balls quite high to make the drill easier; as players gain confidence and comfort with the system, tosses can be more difficult. Make sure to work both sides of the infielder so that she must drop different shoulders when running back. Unless you're locked into another system that works for you, try calling, "Ball, ball" to call for the ball rather than calling, "Mine, mine!" The letter B is phonetically louder and more forceful than the letter M.

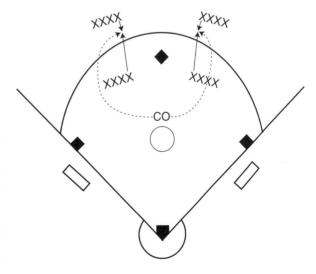

Purpose
To get many reps of ground balls and fly balls without throws

Organization
The defense sets up on a regulation field with bases. Start with all players who play on the left side of the infield in 3B or SS positions and all outfielders in CF and RF. You need two hitters or coaches at home with a large bucket of balls. Give each defensive position an empty bucket for the balls that they field. The second round will reverse, left side to outfielders in LF and CF and all infielders at 2B and 1B.

Execution
Hitters alternate and hit in rapid-fire succession. One hitter hitting from the right-hand side of the batter's box will hit to the right side. The hitter in the left-handed batter's box will hit across the field to the left side. Players will field a ball and then go to the back of the line of players in their position.

Coaching Points
Coaches can mix in ground balls, fly balls, and both forehand and backhand positions. Coaches hitting to the outfield should never hit through or over the infielders. They should keep the balls on the opposite side of the base from the infielders. This is a great drill to get a ton of balls hit to players without taxing their arms. Infielders should always set up as if they are throwing to 1B after they field the ball. Outfielders should always set up their footwork and arm swing as if they are throwing home.

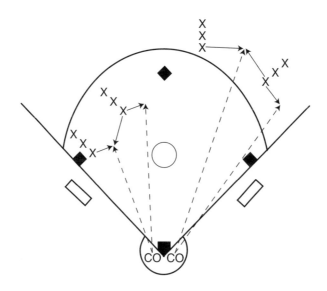

About the Editor

Kirk Walker has been a coach at the NCAA Division I level for more than 20 years. Since his tenure as head softball coach at Oregon State University began in 1995, Walker has accumulated more wins than any other coach in program history. He led the Beavers to eight NCAA tournaments between 1995 and 2006, including the program's first-ever Women's College World Series appearance in 2006. Walker was named the 1999 and 2005 Pac-10 Coach of the Year, the same years his OSU softball staff was named the Speedline/NFCA Pacific Region Coaching Staff of the Year. Walker was a member of the USA Softball National Team coaches pool through the 2004 Olympics. He has served on the executive board of the National Fastpitch Coaches Association since 2003.

Walker came to Oregon State after spending 11 seasons at national powerhouse UCLA as an assistant coach, where he helped lead the Bruins to six NCAA titles and 10 appearances in the College World Series. In the off-season, he also has served as the head coach of the California Commotion, which won the women's major fastpitch national title four consecutive years from 1996 to 1999. He currently resides in Wilsonville, Oregon.

About the Contributors

Louie Berndt was promoted to associate head coach of the Florida State softball program in 2004. First hired as an assistant in 1989, Berndt served one year before becoming head coach at Marshall University. Six years later she returned to Florida State. She has helped lead the Seminoles to seven straight NCAA regional tournaments, including six regional finals and two Women's College World Series appearances from 1999 to 2006. At Marshall, Berndt guided the then-reinstated program to its first-ever Southern Conference Tournament title and first NCAA tournament. She was named the 1996 Southern Conference Coach of the Year. Berndt was a two-time All-American at Western Michigan University.

Carol Bruggeman has been associate head coach at Louisville since 2005. She was an integral member of the 2006 BIG EAST Coaching Staff of the Year, helping guide the Cardinals to a program-best 45-11 record, the regular-season conference title, their first national ranking, and their first appearance in an NCAA regional final. Bruggeman spent 12 years at Purdue, starting the program in 1994 and compiling a 380-304-2 career record. Bruggeman served as an assistant coach at Michigan from 1989 to 1993, during which time the Wolverines won the Big Ten championship and advanced to the NCAA tournament both seasons. Bruggeman began her coaching career as graduate assistant at her alma mater Iowa, where she earned All-Big Ten, All-Mideast Region, and Academic All-America honors as an infielder. She was elected president of the National Fastpitch Coaches Association in 2006.

Yvette Girouard has headed up the Louisiana State University softball program since 2000. She ranks fifth all-time on the NCAA Division I lists for wins and winning percentage, and in 2005 she became the sixth coach in NCAA history to record her 1,000th career victory. Girouard made a clean sweep of the three major Southeastern Conference titles (SEC Western Division, SEC overall, and SEC tournament) in three of her first five seasons as a Tiger, becoming the first coach in league history to lead a team to back-to-back tournament championships. During her two decades as head coach at University of Louisiana at Lafayette

(then Southwestern Louisiana), she was named the National Coach of the Year in 1990 and 1993. Girouard was inducted into the National Fastpitch Coaches Association Hall of Fame in 2005 and the Louisiana Softball Coaches Association Hall of Fame in 2002.

Michelle Gromacki assumed the role of head coach of her alma mater, Cal State Fullerton, in 1999. From 2000 to 2003, she guided her teams to four consecutive Big West Conference championships, bringing the program's total to seven league crowns overall—more than any other school in the history of the conference. The Titans reached the NCAA regional tournament in each of Gromacki's first four seasons and finished in the top 20 in the National Fastpitch Coaches Association's poll in four of her first six seasons. She has been head coach on Speedline/NFCA West Region Coaching Staff of the Year three times and was an assistant coach for

the USA Blue Team in 2001 and the U.S. Elite National Team in 2002 to 2004. As a player, Gromacki helped lead the Titans to a combined 170-19-1 overall record from 1985 to 1987 and to the 1986 NCAA National Championship.

Deanna Gumpf has been the head coach of Notre Dame's softball program since 2002 after serving as an assistant since 1998. From 2002 to 2006, the Irish claimed the BIG EAST Conference regular-season crown four times and the BIG EAST Conference tournament championship three times, and posted a 219-90 record. During that same period, six players earned All-America honors, 24 earned all-BIG EAST recognition, and two were named academic All-America. Gumpf notched her 100th career victory in 2004, reaching the plateau faster than any previous Irish head coach. As an assistant, Gumpf helped the Notre Dame pitching staff

post a 0.89 team ERA in 2001, good for seventh in the nation. Gumpf and her staff were named the conference coaching staff of the year in 2002 and 2004.

Carol Hutchins, the most victorious coach in Michigan Athletics history, has been head coach of the Wolverines softball program since 1985. In 2005, the Maize and Blue became the first program east of the Mississippi River to claim the NCAA championship, and Hutchins was chosen as one of the pool of coaches for USA Softball's Summer Tour. After helping select both the National and Elite Teams for USA Softball in 2005, Hutchins was named head coach of the Elite Team at the Canada Cup and assistant coach of the National Team at the Japan Cup. Hutchins ranks among the top 10 NCAA Division I active coaches in

career wins and winning percentage. She was named the 1995 NFCA National Coach of the Year and was a member of the 2005 Speedline/NFCA National Coaching Staff of the Year. Her teams have earned 10 Big Ten Conference regular-season titles, seven Big Ten Conference tournament championships, and 13 NCAA tournament appearances, including eight trips to the NCAA Women's College World Series.

Kelly Inouye-Perez became the third head coach in UCLA history on January 1, 2007, after spending 17 years in the dugout as a player, assistant coach, and assistant head coach. Inouye-Perez has worked with pitchers and catchers since 1993, when she graduated with a psychology degree after leading the Bruins to three NCAA titles (1989, 1990, and 1992) from behind the plate. The three-time All-Pac-10 selection and member of the 1992 Women's College World Series all-tournament team also was on four national championship teams during her Amateur Softball Association career, and she competed internationally

in the Pan American Games in Japan in 1985 and in Peru in 1987.

Jay Miller has been Mississippi State University's head softball coach since 2002, leading the Bulldogs to the NCAA tournament in his first three seasons. In 2005, he became one of only 14 active Division I coaches to reach the 800-victory milestone. Previously, Miller spent 15 seasons as the head coach at Missouri, where he guided teams to five NCAA tournament appearances, three conference titles, and two trips to the Women's College World Series. Miller is a member of the National Fastpitch Coaches Association All-American committee and a lead instructor for the

NFCA Coaches College. He also was a member of the national team selection committee that formed the team that won gold in the first-ever softball competition in the Olympic Games in 1996.

Teena Murray, director of Olympic sports performance, is in her third year at the University of Louisville. She oversees the strength, conditioning, and performance nutrition programs for all U of L Olympic sports, and works directly with women's soccer, women's basketball, and softball. Murray was named as director of strength and conditioning for the United States Women's Ice Hockey Team in 2006. She also has worked as a consultant for the NHL's Florida Panthers and Mighty Ducks of Anaheim, the Hartford Wolfpack of the American Hockey League, and USA Hockey. Prior to Louisville, Murray was an assistant  strength and conditioning coach at the University of Connecticut for four years and at Cornell University for four years. She is certified by the National Strength and Conditioning Association and United States Weightlifting.

Jennifer Ogee has been an assistant coach at Nebraska since 2001, serving as the hitting coach, working with the catchers and infielders, and coordinating Nebraska's recruiting efforts. From 2002 to 2006, the Cornhuskers' offensive productivity has seen marked improvement and unprecedented consistency in almost every statistical category, and NU advanced to the Women's College World Series in 2002. Formerly Jennifer Cline, Ogee spent four years as an assistant coach at her alma mater, the University of Washington, helping the Huskies advance to the NCAA College World Series every year. Ogee was  the first catcher in UW history, earning All-American and All-WCWS honors and leading the team to a runner-up title in 1996.

Kim Sowder became head coach at Long Beach State following the 2006 season after serving 11 years as assistant and associate coach. Working with hitting and defense, Sowder helped the 49ers post the four highest team batting averages in the history of the program in the 1990s. The 49ers also led the Big West Conference in team fielding percentage for three straight seasons. The former All-American shortstop (1989 to 1992) was inducted into the Long Beach State Athletics Hall of Fame in 1998. Sowder earned her undergraduate degree in marketing in 1993 and then went into the coaching ranks, serving two years as an  assistant coach at Pacific before returning to her alma mater.

Heather Tarr was named head coach at her alma mater, Washington, in 2004 after a six-year stint at Pacific as an assistant and then associate head coach. The Huskies were 70-47 and advanced to the NCAA Super Regionals in her first two years at the helm. In her tenure at Pacific, she was part of the 2001 NFCA West Region Coaching Staff of the Year after guiding the Tigers to within one win of the Women's College World Series and a No. 18 final national ranking. Tarr joined Pacific prior to the 1999 season after an outstanding playing career as a Husky. A four-year letterwinner, Tarr helped lead UW to a second-place finish at the Women's College World Series in 1996 and a third-place finish in 1997.

Michelle Venturella became the first associate head coach in Iowa softball history in 2004. In her first year, Venturella helped the Hawkeyes compile a 44-15 record and win the Big Ten regular-season and tournament championships. As a player, Venturella was one of the best catchers in the country, holding a spot on the U.S. National Team from 1995 to 2000. Throughout her career with USA Softball, she earned four gold medals, including Olympic gold in 2000. She also helped the United States to gold at the 1998 World Championships, and she was an alternate on the 1996 Olympic team. A 1996 graduate of Indiana University, Venturella still ranks among its top five in eight offensive categories and remains Indiana's all-time leader in RBIs and walks.

Margie Wright was the first softball coach to amass 1,000 NCAA Division I career victories, 950 of which have come at Fresno State University. Her remarkable 27-year career includes a national title, six more top-three finishes, 10 regional championships, and 16 conference titles. She has guided the Bulldogs to 10 of the program's 12 NCAA Women's College World Series appearances. Wright also led the USA Softball National Team to a gold medal at the 1998 ISF World Championships. Wright has coached 13 Olympians, 51 All-Americans, 15 academic All-Americans, and two NCAA Top VIII Award Winners. She has been named National Coach of the Year once, Regional Coach of the Year seven times, and West Coast Conference Coach of the Year eight times. Wright is a member of the NFCA Hall of Fame and the Women's Sports Foundation International Hall of Fame.

More resources to help you learn the game's essential skills

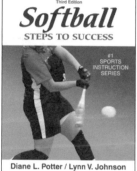
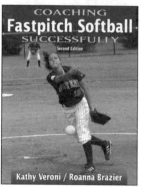